FIGHT BACK

FIGHT BACK

Workplace Justice for Immigrants

Aziz Choudry, Jill Hanley, Steve Jordan,
Eric Shragge, Martha Stiegman
(The Immigrant Workers Centre Research Group)

Fernwood Publishing • Halifax and Winnipeg

Editing: Eileen Young
Cover design: John van der Woude
Cover image: Tatiana Gomez
Printed and bound in Canada by Hignell Book Printing
Printed on paper containing 100% post-consumer fibre.

Published in Canada by Fernwood Publishing
32 Oceanvista Lane
Black Point, Nova Scotia, B0J 1B0
and #8 - 222 Osborne Street, Winnipeg, Manitoba, R3L 1Z3
www.fernwoodpublishing.ca

Fernwood Publishing Company Limited gratefully acknowledges the financial support
of the Government of Canada through the Book Publishing Industry Development
Program (BPIDP), the Canada Council for the Arts and the Nova Scotia
Department of Tourism and Culture for our publishing program.

 Canadian Patrimoine
Heritage canadien
  The Canada Council for the Arts
Le Conseil des Arts du Canada
 NOVA SCOTIA
Tourism and Culture

Library and Archives Canada Cataloguing in Publication

Fight back : work place justice for immigrants / Aziz Choudry ... [et al.].

Includes bibliographical references.
ISBN 978-1-55266-297-7

1. Immigrants--Employment--Canada.
2. Immigrants--Canada--Economic conditions.
3. Immigrants--Canada--Social conditions. I. Choudry, Aziz

HD8108.5.A2F54 2009   331.6'20971   C2008-907765-2

Contents

Contributors

Aziz Choudry is a social activist and an assistant professor in the Department of Integrated Studies in Education at McGill University.

Jill Hanley is an assistant professor in the School of Social Work at McGill University and a co-founder and board member of the Immigrant Workers Centre in Montreal.

Steve Jordan is an assistant professor and chair of the Department of Integrated Studies in Education at McGill University.

Eric Shragge is the principal of the School of Community and Public Affairs at Concordia University and a co-founder of the Immigrants Workers Centre in Montreal.

Martha Stiegman is a filmmaker, activist and PhD candidate in Concordia University's Special Individualized Program.

Acknowledgements

This book is a collaborative product by the authors in conjunction with the Immigrant Workers Centre (IWC) in Montreal. Each of the chapters had a primary author but the whole book was conceived and edited collectively. We wish to acknowledge the contribution of several other people: Lauren Posner and Charlotte Baltodano conducted interviews; Charlotte helped in particular with the group from Latin America and the migrant agricultural workers. Jaggi Singh conducted interviews and put our research team in contact with workers who did not have formal immigration status. Marco Luciano, a co-founder and an organizer at the IWC, was involved at the beginning of the project. He located the people to interview, participated in the interviews and played an important role in helping to build the analysis of the interviews. He introduced the phrase "learning in reverse" to describe the adaptive process experienced by many of those interviewed. Sigalit Gal contributed to the chapter on the Live-In Caregiver Program, and Valérie Lavigne helped with research.

Thanks to everyone involved in the production of this book: Eileen Young for copy editing, Debbie Mathers for inputting the final manuscript changes, Brenda Conroy for design and proofreading and Beverley Rach for production. A special thanks to Errol Sharpe at Fernwood Publishing for all of his support and guidance through the publication process. Finally, thanks to Tatiana Gomez for providing the cover photo and John van der Woude for the cover design.

Acronyms

AAFQ: Association des aides familiales du Quebec

AWA: Agricultural Workers Alliance

BBC: British Broadcasting Corporation

CA4: Canada–Central America Four Free Trade Agreement

CAFTA: Central American Free Trade Agreement

CATTA: Centre d'appui aux travailleurs et travailleuses agricoles

CEGEP: Collège d'enseignement général et professionnel

CCNC: Chinese Canadian National Council

CERIS: Centre of Excellence for Research on Immigration and Settlement

CIC: Citizenship and Immigration Canada

CBC: Canadian Broadcasting Corporation

CIDA: Canadian International Development Agency

CPRMWMF: Convention on the Protection of the Rights of all Migrant Workers and Members of the Families

CSST: Commission de la santé et de la sécurité au travail

EI: Employment Insurance

FARMS: Foreign Agricultural Resource Management Services

FDM: Foreign Domestic Movement

FDNS: Front de défense des non-syndiqués

FERME: Fondation des entreprises en recrutement de main d'œuvre agricole étrangère (Foundation of Companies for the Recruitment of Foreign Agricultural Labour)

FFQ: Fédération des femmes du Quebec

GPB: Government Placement Branch of the Philippines

HR: human resources

HRSDC: Human Resources and Social Development Canada

ICESC: International Covenant on Economic, Social and Cultural Rights

IMA: International Migrants Alliance

IMF: International Monetary Fund

IOM: International Organization for Migration

IWC: Immigrant Workers Centre

IRB: Immigration and Refugee Board

LCP: Live-In Caregiver Program

LCR: Labour Relations Committee

LSPP: Low-Skill Pilot Project

MICC: Ministère de l'immigration et des communautés culturelles

NAFTA: North American Free Trade Agreement

NGO: non governmental organization

OECD: Organisation for Economic Co-operation and Development

PINAY: Filipino Women's Organization in Quebec

POEA: Philippine Overseas Employment Administration

PWC: Philippine Women's Centre of British Columbia

RCMP: Royal Canadian Mounted Police

SAP: Structural Adjustment Program

SAWP: Seasonal Agricultural Worker Program

SAWCC: South Asian Women's Community Centre

SEA: South East Asia

SPP: Security and Prosperity Partnership

SSHRC: Social Science and Humanities Research Council of Canada

TFW: temporary foreign worker

TFWP: Temporary Foreign Worker Program

UFCW: United Food and Commercial Workers

UNDP: United Nations Development Program

UPA: Union des Producteurs Agricoles

USAID: United States Agency for International Development

Chapter 1

Introduction

> I started watching all these relationships, this behaviour; when the supervisor started yelling at me, I told him, listen, I don't need a university degree to do this job, anyone can do this job, so you don't respect me, I don't respect you. So I tried to demand some respect as a worker, as a human being. — a factory worker

One of the major issues currently confronting almost all countries across the planet is that of migration and immigration. Its massive scale today is the result of two interrelated forces — the displacement of people from countries in the South and the demands for cheap labour in the so-called developed North. (Regionally a similar dynamic exists in the South with displacement from less to more advanced capitalist economies: people from Indonesia working in Taiwan exemplifies this phenomenon.) Both the displacement and the demand for labour are connected to a basic restructuring of capitalism arising from the current shift towards liberalized trade and investment and toward the reduction of working-class power through legislation and freeing the market from "state interference." It is important to begin with an analysis of the political and economic context of the massive human displacement that we are witnessing. Fundamentally, it is in the interest of the capitalist class to have a surplus of labour that is competing for work. Both in Canada and elsewhere, to use Marxist terminology, migration and displacement create a huge, mobile and often desperate "reserve army of labour" that competes for jobs, and subsequently becomes a pool of cheap labour that is relatively easy to discipline. The consequence is a large number of workers who face competition and little in the way of protection in the labour market. Although this shapes the context, workers are not necessarily passive in the face of these conditions. This book examines not only the context and the possibilities for fighting back, but also the experiences of immigrant workers themselves.

This book results from the collaboration between a group of university-affili-ated researchers who are all active in different social movements and commu-nity organizations, in partnership with the Immigrant Workers Centre (IWC) in Montreal, and funded through the Social Science and Humanities Research Council (SSHRC).[1] The goal of our research was to document the experiences of immigrant workers in a variety of workplaces: our underlying belief was that the best kind of research tells "how it really is" and comes from the lived experience of people themselves. Interviews were carried out between 2004 and 2006 with approximately fifty workers. Participants had been in Canada for as many as twenty and as little as a two years. We began by interviewing workers who had been active in the IWC, either seeking help there or involved in other aspects of the Centre. We then broadened the interviews to include a group from

Latin America, who had been in Canada for at least ten years. Several from that group came after the 1973 coup in Chile. We also included workers who were in Canada under short-term "guest-worker" programs — such as the Live-In Caregiver Program (LCP) or the Seasonal Agricultural Worker Program (SAWP) . Still others were here in even more precarious positions as refugee claimants or those without any formal status. Many in this final group had little choice about leaving their home countries and faced much discrimination struggling to find their place in Canadian society. Throughout this book, we draw on these interviews to share these experiences and to illustrate broader trends.

The analysis presented in this book, which comes out of this research, also draws on the authors' analysis and reflections resulting from our work with immigrant workers. Several of the authors are involved in the daily activities illustrated in the book, including campaigns, support work and other forms of resistance to the job conditions we describe. The royalties derived from this book will be donated to the IWC.

As engaged researchers, we are concerned not only with analyzing the conditions and issues faced by immigrant workers but also with examining the ways that workers themselves are able to contest these conditions, individually and collectively. One of the first questions we wanted our research to address was why some immigrant workers were able to defend their rights, and resist unjust conditions in their jobs. As we talked to immigrant workers, their stories revealed to us just how complex that question is. We learned about the ongoing adaptation that they undertook to survive the dislocations brought by the international forces of neoliberal globalization (an analysis of this political and economic context follows in the next chapter). The stakes for immigrant workers to succeed in economic terms are very high. They are not only struggling to find a footing in Canada; they must earn enough to support their extended families in their home countries. This is a huge challenge given the barriers they face. The workers we spoke with told us stories of endurance: how their hours were long, how they faced arbitrary discipline and racist comments on the job, and how they received little if any respect from their employers. Many shared with us their stories of fighting back, of moments when they were able to challenge these conditions, sometimes after they were fired or laid off. Many immigrant workers experienced survival and fighting back simultaneously, negotiating the tension between endurance and resistance. People adapted because of economic necessity; they challenged their bosses when their situations became intolerable. Often their acts of resistance and defiance were not motivated by the prospects of material gains, but rather by a demand for basic "respect" or "to be treated as human." Resisting also brought with it the risk, not only of losing the jobs they had, but also of letting down those dependent on the wage they received. For those whose immigration status was inextricably tied to their employer, or for non-status workers, there were added risks of deportation. The narratives in this book are examples of both survival strategies and fighting back.

The Immigrant Workers Centre

The Immigrant Workers Centre (IWC) in Montreal was founded in 2000 by a small group of Filipino-Canadian union and former union organizers, and their allies, comprised of activists and academics. The idea of the Centre grew out of the experience of two of the founders who had worked as union organizers. They observed that much of their recruitment and education to support a union drive had to take place outside of the workplace and there were few places where this could happen, particularly in a collective way. Thus the idea of the Centre was to provide a safe place outside of the workplace where workers could discuss their situation. Further, they had a critique of the unions themselves, arguing that once the unions got a majority to "sign cards" and join the union, the processes of education and solidarity built into the organizing process were lost, as union "bureaucrats" came in to manage the collective agreement. In its first year, the organization was able to secure a grant from the Social Justice Fund of the Canadian Automobile Workers to intervene on labour issues in the community. The IWC then got to work providing ongoing education and a critical analysis that goes beyond the specific role of unions, as well as finding ways to address worker issues outside of the traditional union structures.

The activities of the IWC include individual rights counselling, as well as popular education and political campaigns that reflect the general issues facing immigrant workers, such as dismissal, problems with employers or, sometimes, inadequate representation by their unions. Labour education is a priority, targeting organizations in the community and increasing workers' skills and analysis. Workshops on themes such as the history of the labour movement, the *Labour Standards Act* and collective organizing processes have been presented in many organizations that work with immigrants as well as at the IWC itself. The "Skills for Change" program teaches basic computer literacy, while incorporating workplace analysis and information on rights. The goal is to integrate specific computer skills while supporting individuals in becoming more active in defending labour rights in their workplaces. There is also an ongoing link between the struggles of immigrant workers with other social and economic struggles; building alliances is a priority. In addition, the IWC supports union organizing in workplaces where there is a high concentration of immigrant workers.

Campaigns are viewed not only as a way to make specific gains for immigrant workers but also as a way to educate the wider community about the issues that they face. For example, the first campaign, in 2000, was formed to defend a domestic worker, who had entered Canada under the Live-In Caregiver Program, against deportation. In addition to winning the campaign, the issue of importing labourers as "indentured servants" was brought into the public sphere: as a result, many community organizations and unions became involved in this issue. Because many immigrant workers do not work in unionized shops, the *Labour Standards Act* provides one of the few recourses for non-unionized workers in disputes with their employers. Along with many other groups in Quebec, the IWC became involved in a campaign to reform the *Labour Standards Act* in 2002.

The IWC used the campaign to raise specific concerns, including the exclusion of domestic workers from this Act, and the difficulty faced by these workers in accessing information on their rights. The IWC actively contributed to the campaign, using the campaign to educate, mobilize and organize immigrant workers. In 2003, several victories were won, including the coverage of domestic workers by the reformed *Labour Standards Act*. However, despite the reforms won in this province-wide campaign, the Act still fails in many ways to protect workers in precarious and irregular jobs.

Another aspect of the IWC's work has been its contribution to the organizing of cultural events with political content. The first was an International Women's Day event organized in 2001. A coalition of immigrant women of diverse origins organized a cultural event, panels and a march to emphasize the concerns of immigrant women in Canada, as well as international solidarity. This event has become an annual event: its success has increased the profile of issues faced by immigrant women within the wider women's movement in Quebec. The first Mayworks event, a community/union festival celebrating labour struggles through the arts, was launched for May Day of 2005. The festival, initiated by the IWC, found collaboration from trade unions and the wider activist community. Two concerts and a community event in a park marked the event. The event has been held annually since then.

Overall, the IWC is a place of intersection between the traditions of labour and community movements. Traditionally, work-related issues have been the concern of the labour movement, acting on the assumption that the best way for workers to have a strong voice is through the union movement. However, the IWC, along with other organizations, sees that union representation is limited because of the difficulties in organizing immigrant workers discussed above. New forms of labour organizing are required in the current context that include both support for and from the trade union movement. The IWC works at both levels with the goals of serving, organizing and educating those who are not unionized. At the same time that it supports worker efforts to unionize, it also helps them get adequate services from their unions. The union-community relationship is developed through many activities of the Centre, including building alliances with younger union activists, as well as supporting immigrants in organizing and in helping them negotiate conflicts with their trade unions.

The work of the IWC has formed new alliances and its office has become a meeting place for many groups of social activists. The core of the organization is a group made up of immigrant union and labour organizers and allies who have been active on both labour and community issues for many years. In addition, the IWC is connected to student and anti-globalization activists. There are several reasons for this. The centre has been fortunate to have student placements from law, social work and related fields from several Montreal universities and colleges. Many of these students have been involved in student organizing: this has helped to connect students to the issues raised by the IWC. In addition, students have found the IWC to be a setting that offers them an opportunity to combine radical politics and local work. At the same time, the IWC's connection with these groups has helped to clarify its own positions on broader social issues. The IWC is a place that brings together union, community and student activists, and people of different ages, ethnic, cultural and class backgrounds to work for social justice for immigrant workers.

Overview of the Book

This book brings together experiences of immigrant workers, their stories of adaptation to Canadian society and their experiences with defending their rights and resisting injustices, mainly at work. Chapter 2 presents a broad contextualization of immigration to Canada. It provides an overview of the history of Canada as a "white settler colonial state" and of the role of immigrant labour as one of the key ingredients necessary to "build" the society. The current neoliberal context is explored in order to situate the forces that push people to leave their countries and come to Canada. The chapter surveys the situations facing immigrant workers that these global neoliberal forces construct. Understanding the context is the beginning of an analysis of barriers and opportunities to challenge them.

In Chapter 3, we turn to the experiences of immigrant workers and explore the process we term "becoming an immigrant worker." Drawing from the interviews, we share workers' stories of leaving their countries, of settling in Canada and of their situations at work. These stories reflect how the wider economic and political forces shape the choices for immigrant workers, the pressures to leave their countries of origin, the choice of employment and the lack of options that ties them to low-wage work.[2]

Chapter 4 examines the issues of policy and rights. In theory, Canada offers the same rights and services to all workers: they are supposed to have equal access to regulatory bodies when the legislated norms are violated. In practice, as our interviews make clear, this is not the case. Labour standards, workers' compensation, employment insurance, access to education and recognition of credentials all function to keep immigrant workers ghettoized in low wage work. Further, it is difficult for many immigrants to learn about and act on their rights because of discrimination and racist practices.

As Canada moves toward adopting broad programs of importing workers on a temporary basis to fill particular jobs in areas such as construction and tourism, it is important to understand that such temporary labour mobility programs have been in operation in Canada for decades, particularly the Seasonal Agricultural Worker Program (SAWP) and the Live-In Caregiver Program (LCP). Chapters 5 and 6 examine those programs. In each chapter we present the wider policy context of these programs, the experiences of the workers in them and finally the forms of resistance and organizing of these workers and their fight against specific working conditions, as well the policy structure of the programs themselves.

Chapter 7 presents the dual experiences of immigrant workers, enduring and surviving the brutal realities of immigration and work, while and at the same time fighting back and challenging them. We do not see these two concepts — survival and fighting back — as being in a binary opposition. They are processes people live and experience simultaneously. The chapter presents some of the resistance stories in more detail. We conclude with political lessons — political in the sense that immigrant workers and their organizations are challenging both the power of employers and the wider government policies that shape the unjust situations of immigrant workers. We end with lessons drawn from these experiences.

Notes

1. The grant was entitled The Changing Nature of Work in the New Economy: National and Case Study Perspectives, SSHRC-Major Collaborative Research Initiatives Program- Project No. 512-2001-1011, covering 2003–2007.
2. All names of migrant and immigrant workers have been changed out of concern for their job security.

Chapter 2

Context

> In the age of globalization, the world is indeed becoming smaller and easier to traverse — for capital and for those who manage and represent its interests. But for those who labor, the nation and its borders have thicker walls. To them, national boundaries sometimes seem as formidable and impenetrable as the barbed wire surrounding a prison. (Biju Mathew 2005: 146)

Despite growing academic, public and political focus on migration and immigration in recent years, neither globalization, migration nor the struggles of immigrant workers for justice and dignity are new phenomena, in Canada or internationally. British author and antiracist activist Teresa Hayter (2000) outlines four periods of major migrations during the capitalist era since the sixteenth century. The first was the forced migration through slavery from Africa to the Americas for mine and plantation labour, after the genocide wrought against Indigenous Peoples in the western hemisphere facilitated the acquisition of their lands and resources. The second mass migration comprised indentured/bonded labour, whereby temporary slaves from India and China were often effectively forced into highly exploitative contracts for a minimum of ten years in numerous countries in other parts of Asia, Africa, the Pacific Islands, the Caribbean and Latin America. Many returned to their countries of origin; many others remained in the countries in which they were brought to work, some unable to afford the return home. The third period of migration was that of millions of Europeans emigrating to the Americas, Australia, Aotearoa/New Zealand and Central/Southern Africa, starting in the eighteenth century. The fourth period was a flow of migration from the global South to the North, starting in the 1950s, at a time of post-war industrial expansion and labour shortages.

These four periods of migrations are reflected in Canadian history. It is important to locate our analysis of the material conditions and struggles of immigrant workers in Canada today in a wider geo-historical context and in reference to the process of construction of the Canadian nation. Since colonization, the nation-state of Canada has been based on the creation of a settler colony primarily for British and French immigrants, built on the dispossession of Indigenous Peoples and the commodification and appropriation of their lands and resources, and constructed with successive waves of immigrant labour. The ongoing colonization and dispossession of Indigenous Peoples underpins the very existence of the Canadian nation-state. As feminist scholar/activist Sunera Thobani notes, the nation-state and Canadian citizenship remain highly racialized constructs which are mapped to European/white identity and power.

Gada Mahrouse (2006) writes of a "pervasive racialized hegemony that is central to nation-building in Canada" (449). This racialized hegemony under-pins immigration and labour market policies. As a number of scholars (Chang 2000; Thobani 2000, 2007; Abu-Laban and Gabriel 2002) argue, contemporary Canadian immigration, labour and other policy frameworks maintain a regime where different categories of workers enjoy deeply unequal rights. New immigrants, temporary migrant workers and non-status people living in Canada are defined with reference to a hierarchy of immigration categories: they also face cross-cutting injustices, sometimes regardless of their status. Their accounts, in the form of interviews and vignettes about their experiences, are woven throughout this book.

Like other western countries, Canada has long maintained racialized immigration policies — first explicitly so, and then more subtly through other categories and approaches such as points-based systems and inadequate funding for language training, which more subtly discriminated in favour of Anglophone and Francophone immigrants from the "developed" world. Notwithstanding the fact that there have been significant longstanding Black and Asian communities in different parts of Canada, immigration policy was for the most part a de facto "whites only" one until the 1960s. Thobani notes that Canada's current immigration policy and state-building practices relied on

> the acquisition of the "national" territory through the colonization and racialization of Aboriginal peoples, and on the producing of a "national" population by legally distinguishing between "preferred" and "non-preferred" race immigrants, with the former being drawn into settlement and reproduction of the nation and the latter being discouraged from permanent settlement, having been constructed as a threat to the "purity" and "whiteness" of the nation. (2000: 281)

Kamat, Mir and Mathew (2004) concur that nation-states are not created through some organic, natural process over time, but are constituted through specific practices. Among these,

> the notion of citizenship is clearly central to deciding who belongs or does not belong, and how these categories are to be managed and governed differ in each historical period. The identification of certain individuals (or groups) as citizens and the exclusion of certain others are acts of power that establish the sovereignty of a nation state and define the rights of a State over particular bodies in particular ways. (Kamat, Mir and Mathew 2004: 18)

David McNally argues that it is not the case that global business does not want immigrant labour to enter the West, but that it "simply wants this labour on its own terms: frightened, oppressed, vulnerable. The fundamental truth about globalization — that it represents freedom for capital and unfreedom for labour — is especially clear where global migrants are concerned" (2002: 137).

Canada has historically used a racialized immigration policy to provide the labour of immigrants to the national economy. Although, between the 1970s and 1990s, immigration was ostensibly liberalized, now the regime has become more restrictive again. Parallels and indeed continuities exist that link the overt racism of past immigration policies to current policy moves and selection criteria, which many critics argue are racist as well as gendered.

The 1885 *Chinese Immigration Act* required Chinese workers recruited to build Canada's railways to pay a $50 head tax each. In 1903, this amount was increased to $500 (equivalent to two houses) and Chinese workers were deemed ineligible for family reunification or citizenship, while European immigrants were granted immediate citizenship and given land. For many years, Chinese were regarded as the least popular of all potential immigrants to Canada. In 1923, legislation ended the Head Tax, but also blocked all but a few Chinese from immigrating to Canada (CCNC 2009). Before 1947, discriminatory immigration laws made it impossible for all but a few Chinese men, and very few women, to live permanently in Canada. Between 1946 and 1950, Chinese immigrants constituted only 0.6 percent of total immigration to Canada. For a long time before 1997, the number of Chinese immigrants remained small (Tan and Roy 1985). The experience of early Chinese immigrants to Canada illustrates that the history of Canadian immigration is also gendered; the exclusion of Chinese women in the late nineteenth and early twentieth centuries for fear of contamination of racial purity prefigures more recent restrictions on family class immigrants that also disproportionately impact women.

Since the 1970s, the numbers of immigrants arriving from European countries has steadily declined while there has been an increase in immigrants arriving from countries in the Caribbean, Central and South America, Africa, the Middle East and Asia. According to Statistics Canada (1996: 1–2) prior to 1961 about 90 percent of immigrants arrived from Europe, but between 1991 and 1996, only 19 percent came from European countries and 57 percent from Asia. With the 1984 Parliamentary Committee report *Equality Now*, the issue of racial discrimination became a prominent part of contemporary scholarship. The Report of the Equality in Employment Commission identified racial discrimination in employment as a serious issue that needed addressing.

In the late twentieth and early twenty-first centuries, dominant narratives of Canadian immigration tend to claim that race-based immigration policies have come to an end and have been replaced by "multicultural" practices (Canadian Heritage website). An image of Canada has been constructed that portrays the nation and national values as inherently humanitarian and caring (Razack 2004; Mahrouse 2006; Thobani 2007). Moreover, a number of critical academic readings (Arat-Koç 1999; Abu-Laban and Gabriel 2002; Thobani 2000, 2007) contend that the introduction of the immigration points system and the end to explicit discrimination in favour of "white" immigrants to Canada by no means deracialized immigration policy; nor, more broadly, do these policy changes substantively trouble understandings of who and what is "Canada" and

"Canadian" or challenge the "hegemonic Euro-Canadian project" (Thobani 2007: 16). Equally, the everyday worlds of immigrant workers, non-status people and Indigenous Peoples in Canada and struggles for justice seriously challenge the notion of Canada as an altruistic, just and inclusive society.

Immigration in a Neoliberal Era:
From the Head Tax to the Points System

Since the 1970s, capitalist restructuring has negatively impacted labour and workers' rights worldwide, including in Canada. Unionized public and private sector jobs, especially in manufacturing are being replaced by casualized, part-time and more poorly paid service jobs, as much production is shifted to sites in the Third World.

Abu-Laban and Gabriel (2002) and Arat-Koç (1999) draw attention to the way in which the increasing neoliberalism underpinning Canadian government policy has impacted on immigration policy. Under a neoliberal regime, the state role in regulating the labour market is changing: the state and the economy are also undergoing extensive restructuring. New immigrants to Canada are increasingly viewed as potential contributors to Canada's "global competitiveness": in a time of fiscal restraint, they are expected to be self-sufficient agents who must shoulder increased responsibilities for adaptation and integration.

Abu-Laban and Gabriel note:

> On the one hand, the state has moved from trying to actively manage some aspects of the economy through immigration policy. For example, Canada is abandoning the practice of matching immigrants to particular labour market niches. On the other, the Canadian state is maintaining and reasserting its control over those categories deemed less desirable, such as women (in the family class) and refugees. With the costs of integration increasingly privatized, the state has more flexibility to cut existing immigrant settlement services. (2002: 97)

For landed immigrants, the introduction in 1995 of a $975 "right-of-landing" fee constituted a further step towards the privatization of immigration and the withdrawal of state responsibilities towards new migrants: in effect it became a new form of head tax. This placed a further obstacle on migrants coming from low-income countries. Although the Harper government reduced this fee by 50 percent in 2006, its 2008 amendments to the *Immigration and Refugee Protection Act* have been roundly criticized by a range of immigrant and refugee rights groups and other community organizations for handing sole power and discretion to the Minister of Immigration to make decisions about which categories of immigrants should enter Canada and from which countries of origin: this legislation effectively discourages family reunification (CBC 2008).

Arat-Koç (1999) and Abu-Laban and Gabriel (2002) note how Canadian government discourse in recent immigration policies is couched in economic terms, "emphasizing how immigrants may be affecting Canadian economic performance and whether and how much they cost the welfare state" (Arat-Koç 1999: 41). Arat-Koç notes that "whatever the actual causes or motivations might be for the state to create unequal categories of citizenship/non-citizenship, the categories themselves correspond to gender, age and other inequalities that prevail in society" (Arat-Koç: 38). Biases embedded in immigration and citizenship policies as to who are "deserving" and "undeserving" immigrants are exaggerated in the current neoliberal policy era. The notion of family-class immigrant contributions to Canadian society and community is based on assumptions about participation in the labour market; it is also highly gendered. This amounts to the commodification of immigrants. or as Arat-Koç puts it, "an evaluation of people's potential contribution to and value to the country solely on the basis of their expected place in the labour market" (Arat-Koç 1999: 36).

Abu-Laban and Gabriel (2002) contend that

> employment equity has been subverted by the emergence of new neo-liberal norms associated with a discourse of globalization. These norms emphasize minimal state action in the economy and privilege the market; they offer narrower understandings of equality, which effectively reject group-based claims.... The emerging voluntary "equal opportunities" plans and "managing diversity" models in firms tend to focus on how diversity can help to secure the bottom line. In this case, diversity is viewed as favorable in relation to competitiveness both at home and abroad. These market-orientated constructions of diversity effectively displace issues of systemic discrimination. (158)

Faith is placed in the market to deliver equitable outcomes in terms of labour-market inequalities. Neoliberal values guide new policy directions in immigration, multiculturalism and employment equity. Abu-Laban and Gabriel join others who point to a process of commodification of minorities and minority cultures arguing that, effectively and literally, multiculturalism means business.

With the intensification and restructuring of capitalism has come an intensification of inequality. The International Labour Organization (2002) partly attributes the significant rise in irregular forms of migration and the irregular status of an estimated 15 percent or more of migrant workers to "the increasing commercialization of the private recruitment process and the growing practice among developed countries of applying unduly restrictive immigration policies" (International Labour Organization 2002). Canada is no exception. Neoliberalism has shaped and expanded immigration policy to include various forms of what are essentially guest-worker programs and broader approaches to immigration such as the points system. Ottawa is devolving state responsibility for settling new immigrants onto community groups and individual immigrants, while facilitating the increased privatization — greater employer/private-sector involvement — through temporary foreign worker programs.

Canada's Brand of Global Capitalism Pushes People to Migrate

> The aliens who present themselves at the Canadian borders today come from countries that are among the most coveted sites for the operations of Canadian corporations. Many of these are also the destinations of the high-flying trade missions led by a dizzying array of prime ministers and trade ministers. (Sunera Thobani 2007: 71)

Canadian governments and big business have benefited greatly from colonial relations of exploitation, whether as part of the British Empire, the Western Alliance during the Cold War and/or the G8 in more recent times. These colonial relations are now locked in and exacerbated by international financial, economic and trade agreements. In addition to the neoliberal underpinning of domestic policy, in international forums such as the Organisation for Economic Cooperation and Development (OECD) and the World Trade Organization (WTO), Canada is a significant supporter of free-market capitalist policies — not least in agriculture — which have destroyed or eroded traditional societies and livelihood opportunities in the name of a model of development emphasizing export-driven, market-oriented growth.

Migration is shaped by interconnected "push" and "pull" factors. Push factors include structural adjustment programs imposed by the World Bank/International Monetary Fund and other financial institutions, and often supported through bilateral official aid, "development" projects and the restructuring of economies along neoliberal lines through trade and aid arrangements. Justin Akers Chacón writes of "neoliberal immigration" — "displacement accompanied by disenfranchisement and often internal segregation in host countries" (2006: 90). Neoliberal policies force people from their farms, jobs, families and communities, pushing them into exploitation and precarity as migrant workers in other countries. Deindustrialization and the downsizing and privatization of essential services — accompanied by increasing user fees — are other "push factors," forcing growing numbers to seek work abroad. Health and education professionals in shattered public sectors are forced to migrate in search of work. The material conditions in workers' countries of origin, as well as the structures of labour markets in the migrant-receiving countries shape the place of migrant workers. Free-trade and investment agreements such as NAFTA and structural adjustment programs push farmers off their land as common lands are privatized — often to facilitate corporate export-based agricultural production. This forces people in the Americas into low-wage labour in *maquiladora* assembly plants; alternatively, they must find ways to migrate north across an increasingly dangerous and militarized U.S.–Mexico border. Likewise, the activities of Canadian mining corporations in the Philippines, India, Colombia and other parts of the world, which have both shaped and benefited from deregulated natural resources policies, have led to displacement and the impoverishment of entire communities, who are often forced to migrate and seek livelihoods elsewhere. At the same time both short-term guest-worker programs and the promise of a "better life" attract workers to advanced capitalist countries like Canada. However, as the stories in the second chapter of this volume illustrate, the reality often does not live up to the promise.

As Razack (2004), Thobani (2007) and others contend, Canada's role in creating or exacerbating these push factors needs close scrutiny. Hayter observes that worldwide "many of the most recent economic migrants... are from Asian countries where there has been rapid industrialization, and where private foreign investment has both created links with industrialized countries and broken links with traditional methods of making a living" (2000: 8). The economies of countries as diverse as Mexico, the Philippines, Pakistan and Bangladesh have become increasingly dependent on remittances in the wake of the loss of foreign-exchange earning capacity, takeovers by privatization and massive public sector cuts. Sutcliffe observes that "the individual decisions of individual migrant workers lead to considerably more money being transferred to poorer countries than all the development aid provided by the world's richest countries (including the multilateral agencies)" (2004: 273). Migrant workers and remittances are a key area of interest to the World Bank, the European Commission, the International Organization for Migration (IOM) and other international agencies, which increasingly promote the concept of migrant workers' family remittances to keep their native countries from collapsing. Remittances are what Devesh Kapur calls "the new development mantra" (2004: 1).

Despite the rhetoric of globalization, there has been a tendency to see increasingly more restrictive immigration policies and practices in western countries. Saskia Sassen suggests that "economic globalization denationalizes national economies; in contrast, immigration is renationalizing politics" (1996: 59). Richmond describes the rise of "a system of global apartheid based on discrimination against migrants and refugees from poorer developing countries" (1994: 204).

While migration and movement of peoples are phenomena as old as humanity itself, recent dynamics of immigration are characteristic of modern global capitalism. With the intensification of neoliberal globalization comes an increased likelihood of larger numbers of "environmental" refugees as climate change disproportionately affects people in the Third World. This follows on from earlier waves of people being displaced by infrastructure megaprojects and development fads such as dams, aquaculture, mines, highways and plantation forestry. Looking towards 2050, a 2007 United Nations Population Division report predicts that migration — mainly from Africa and Asia and countries of the former Communist bloc — is likely to dramatically increase populations in the "developed" world, where ageing populations would have otherwise stagnated or declined were it not for immigration (U.N. Department of Economic and Social Affairs 2007).

(In)Security Climate

Well before the September 11, 2001, attacks on the World Trade Center and the Pentagon, "national security" ideology had already been invoked in Canada to regulate who crosses which borders, and under what conditions they are allowed to live in Canada (Thobani 2007; Kinsman et al. 2000). This has been articulated through policy positions informed by arguments for (Euro-Canadian) racial purity and eugenics, the internment and forced labour of thousands of Ukrainian, Italian and German immigrants from 1914–1920, the appalling treatment of Canadians of Japanese origin in the internment camps during World War II, the Cold War paranoia about communism creeping into Canada with Eastern European immigrants in the early part of the twentieth century and now through the painting of Muslim communities as either dangerous men or imperiled women in need of saving (Thobani 2007; Razack 2008). The concept of national security is very elastic, infused with xenophobia and adaptable to the prevailing state ideology. It can be stretched to fit whatever the "threat of the day" is. Some commentators construct Canada's national security policies as involving little more than buckling to U.S. pressure; but the current anti-Muslim climate echoes state ideological practices found in relation to communities targeted by Canadian governments in previous decades. It is important to understand these policies as having a domestic foundation, within Canada, and not merely as a case of a smaller, benign, humane country being pushed around by its more powerful southern neighbour.

September 11, 2001 was a pretext to push through with a number of measures impacting immigration. In December 2002, Canada and the U.S. signed the Safe Third Country Agreement, which enforced the notion that once an asylum claimant has made a case in one country, and presumably has had a fair hearing, he or she should not be entitled to make a claim in another country. This agreement was strongly criticized by refugee advocates on both sides of the Canada–U.S. border as being detrimental to the safety and rights of refugee claimants (see Canadian Council for Refugees 2008, website).

In Quebec, the rhetoric of *accommodements raisonnables* (reasonable accommodation) and the recent *Bouchard-Taylor Consultation Commission on Accommodation Practices Related to Cultural Differences* by the Quebec provincial government adds another layer to the anti-immigrant (and more specifically, anti-Muslim) climate. It places a certain construction of white Quebecois as the norm and has provided a (state-sanctioned) platform for xenophobia in the guise of an open, frank and democratic public discussion (Choudry, Mahrouse and Shragge 2008). With the media sensationalization of actual or perceived Muslim traditions and cultural/religious practices, little discussion has been had about the problems of learning French when you work sixteen-hour days in a factory six days a week or long hours as a domestic worker — especially given the cutting back of services like language classes to new immigrants or new limits placed on eligibility for such schemes.

Multiculturalism and Diversity

Thobani (2007) argues that state multiculturalism has allowed for the detaching, sidelining and erasure of antiracist action, giving the state (and white Canadian publics) the right to define and keep in their place, non-white Canadians and immigrants. This also undermines Indigenous Peoples' demands for justice, further marginalizing them within the "new multicultural mosaic" of Canada.

The state and provincial governments have done little to address anti-immigrant sentiment and are themselves implicated in renewed targeting of certain communities (e.g., Muslim, Arab and South Asian) and of certain categories of immigrant workers (e.g., non-status). Indeed the dominant conception of diversity emphasizes the economic or potential economic contribution of individuals as the sum worth of a person: she/he is seen as a trade-enhancing commodity. Diversity becomes something to be commodified, consumed, capitalized upon or marketed. As Abu-Laban and Gabriel put it, in the policy areas of immigration, multiculturalism and employment equity "the focus on economic rationalism has rendered a profoundly narrow vision of diversity, which is basically a selling-out of an agenda based on pursuing substantive equality for those marginalized by race/ethnicity, gender, and class" (2002: 173).

Guest Workers

Perhaps nowhere is the categorization, regulation and racialization of work in Canada more obvious than in temporary worker programs such as the Live-In Caregiver Program (LCP), which brings in caregivers, mainly from the Philippines, and the Seasonal Agricultural Worker Program (SAWP). In these programs there is a clear distinction between the civil rights of foreigners and those of citizens. As already suggested, the social, political and economic exclusion and "othering" of temporary/non-status/recent immigrant workers is intrinsic to Canadian national formation. Jobs that were initially done by white Canadians, new European immigrants who were granted status, were filled by non-white workers. By contrast, the non-white temporary workers in these categories are, for the most part, denied the automatic right of permanent residency, freedom of movement between employers and jobs, and access to rights and entitlements of social citizenship.

A number of countries, perhaps most notably Germany, have maintained immigration/labour regimes that created often sizeable numbers of "guest workers." These workers are not granted citizenship and are often tied to a specific employer through a combination of their immigration and labour permits. Canada's SAWP, LCP and the new Temporary Foreign Worker Program (TFWP) regulate the distinctions made between the rights of temporary workers and those of permanent residents. Canada, along with other countries, is moving to expand these programs, with greater involvement of the private sector and international organizations such as the International Organization for Migration (IOM). It is doing this in spite of criticisms of such programs and the accompanying injustices and inequalities in both the workplace and wider society experienced by new immigrants and racialized communities in Canada.

In guest-worker and temporary migrant worker schemes, migrant workers are commodities, temporary labour units to be recruited, utilized and sent away again in accordance with the requirements of employers. Temporary workers, tied to a particular employer, are therefore often stuck with worse conditions than regular workers and have little recourse to improve them. Temporary/guest-worker schemes are essentially a "just-in-time" mechanism to deliver workers and production to the Canadian economy. We now see a renewed interest and reinvigoration of the maintenance and reworking of policies to exploit migrant workers and construct them as an underclass of non-citizens.

More Than Just Another Statistic? Recent Trends

> A lot of Filipinos and others are silent in their jobs.... They don't say anything in their jobs even if they are exploited because they are scared. They are scared that if they do something for change, they will be deported, especially those who are in the Live-In Caregiver Program, and even those with immigrant status. They are scared to be terminated. They feel held at the blade between life and death. — Filipino-Canadian labour organizer

A January 2007 Statistics Canada report examining the economic welfare of immigrant families found no improvement for the economic situation of new immigrants to Canada at the start of the twenty-first century. This was despite the fact that they had much higher levels of education and many more were in the skilled immigrant class than a decade earlier. The report assesses their economic situation since 2000 and the extent of "chronic" low income, as well as the impact of changes in education and skill classes on their economic well-being since 1993. In 2002, low-income rates among immigrants during their first full year in Canada were 3.5 times higher than those of Canadian-born people. By 2004, these had edged down to 3.2 times higher. These rates were higher than at any time during the 1990s, when they were around three times higher than rates for Canadian-born people. The increase in low income was concentrated among immigrants who had been here only one or two years. This suggests that they have had more problems adjusting over the short-term during the years since 2000. The report found that, overall, the large increase in educational attainment of new immigrants, and the shift to the skilled class immigrant, had only a small impact on their likelihood of not being in a low-income category (Statistics Canada, January 2007, The Daily).

Citing Picot and Hou, Statistics Canada (January 2007) states: "In the three major immigrant-receiving cities (Toronto, Vancouver and Montreal) virtually all of the increase in the cities' low-income rate during the 1990s was concentrated among the immigrant population" (10). The growth of the racialized population far outpaced that of the Canadian population in the 1996–2001 census period, especially in urban areas and in Alberta, B.C., Ontario and Quebec.

A Statistics Canada report notes that:

> The movement to having *more highly educated immigrants* and the shift to accepting more *skilled class immigrants* had only a small effect. Regarding education, the differences in the probability of the outcomes between

the less and more highly educated is not as great as one might expect. Furthermore, the advantage that the more highly educated had in the early 1990s was reduced by 2000, as their numbers increased, and after 2000, as economic conditions in the technology sector declined. (Picot, Hou and Coulombe 2006: 34)

Teelucksingh and Galabuzi note:

> Skilled migrants are attracted from their home countries by an aggressive immigration policy which promises the potential to improve their lives and be successful contributors to a modern economy and multicultural society. Many then find themselves relegated to precarious employment in low wage sectors and low end occupations because barriers in the Canadian economy deny them the opportunity to attain employment and compensation commensurate with their training and experience. (2005: 5)

During the period of 1996–2001, Teelucksingh and Galabuzi note that

> racialized group members and new immigrants experienced a median after-tax income gap of 13.3% and an average after-tax income gap of 12.2 %. The gap was highest among male youth (average after-tax income gap 42.3% and median after-tax income gap 38.7%), as well as those with less than high school education (median after-tax income gap 20.6%) and those over 65 years (average income gap 28% and median income gap 21%).

Canada pursues aggressive recruiting of skilled migrants through immigration but its laissez-faire approach to integration leaves new immigrants struggling. Well-educated immigrants are supposed to be the future of Canada's increasingly labour-strapped economy. With massive baby boom retirements on the horizon, and without new immigrant workers, it is unclear who will pay pensions and keep tax dollars flowing for social programs for Canadians in their old age (Teelucksingh and Galabuzi 2005: 8).

According to a Conference Board of Canada (2004) study, racialized groups averaged less than 11 percent of the labour force between 1992–2000 but accounted for 0.3 percent of real gross domestic product (GDP) growth. This starkly contrasts with the remaining 89 percent of the Canadian labour force that contributed 0.6 percent, yet this productivity was not rewarded, since average wages for racialized groups during this period were 14.5 percent lower than that of other Canadians (Conference Board of Canada 2004).

Quebec and Montreal

A study for Le Forum régional sur le développement social (February 2007) found that newly arrived immigrants in Montreal are the group with the highest risk of living in poverty. Based on 2001 statistics, 47.4 percent are living below the low-income threshold. The report states that even after they have been here for over ten years 40 percent of this group will still live below the low-income threshold.

According to a Statistics Canada report, Quebec was the second most popular province destination for new immigrants and Montreal was the second most popular census metropolitan area (after Toronto). New immigrants in Montreal fared less well in the labour market than their counterparts in other census metropolitan areas like Toronto and Vancouver (Tran and Chu 2006).

Education

> During the process of looking for a job, I found that past working experience is not acknowledged in Canada.... What disappoints me a little bit is the discrimination. I thought Canada is an immigrant country and immigrants will be treated equally. But my experience told me discrimination is everywhere.
> —Chinese woman

> Canada has not given me anything in the education sense. I have my diplomas that are not worth anything here. I would have to start from scratch.
> —Mexican worker

Li, Gervais and Duval (2006) cite three main challenges for immigrants in finding employment in Montreal: lack of Canadian work experience, lack of acceptance or recognition of their foreign work experience or qualifications and language barrier. They note that immigrants who have been in Canada for ten years or less are twice as likely as Canadian-born workers to experience over-qualification and twice as likely to stay overqualified 100 percent of the time. Fifty-two percent of recent immigrants with university degrees worked in a job requiring only high school education at some point during a six-year period — almost twice the proportion of 28 percent among Canadian-born counterparts.

Our interviews strongly corroborated official statistics regarding the lack of recognition for skills and training — another key obstacle for immigrants in Canada, which calls into question the construction of Canada as being an inclusive, just, welcoming society for new immigrants from across the world. Academic and professional qualifications and prior job experience in the immigrant's country of origin were frequently dismissed as irrelevant. Facing a long, expensive and humiliating option to seek qualifications in Canada, while often under pressure to begin earning as soon as possible, highly qualified immigrants find themselves in menial poorly paid jobs, often with very difficult working conditions. Harold Bauder, commenting on the role of professional organizations in de-skilling immigrants and the mismatch between immigration-selection procedures and the recognition of foreign credentials, is worth citing at length:

> The devaluation of foreign education and credentials and the demand for Canadian experience are viewed by institutional administrators

as major barriers to labour-market integration among Canadian immigrants. Due to this barrier, immigrants suffer from occupational downgrading, are forced to switch careers and experience loss of social status. Many immigrants feel that they have been tricked into this situation by Canadian immigration policies and labour-market regulations that do not disclose to immigrants prior to their arrival in Canada that their human capital will be devaluated.... Canadian professionals collectively use the practice of credential assessment to reserve employment in these occupations for themselves. Professional organizations constitute an institutional element in the critical infrastructure that imposes a separate set of rules onto their own segment of the labour market, enforcing the reproduction of a professional class of Canadians. (Bauder 2003: 713)

This process has devastating consequences for new immigrants, as their skills are devalued or denied altogether, limiting their opportunity to make a decent living, and undermining their dignity. As skilled persons emigrating from their country of origin, they are already part of a "brain drain." When their qualifications and experience count for nothing in Canada, they become part of another kind of brain drain. Shen, a Chinese man with an engineering degree, works at a delivery job in a restaurant, a significant step down from the social standing he enjoyed in China. He says:

I am a senior official in government in China. What I did now is a labour job with low income. I belong to the lowest class here... Immigrants will never go to the upper level in this country.

Fertile Soil for Struggle?

Seasonal workers provide the core 18 percent of the agricultural workforce which does much of the dirty, dangerous and repetitive manual work that sustains the horticulture industry. (Gibb 2006: 5)

They look down on us. But the Quebecers, when they finish their contract, the government pays them all winter long. But us, who pays us all winter? We have to pay our own bills at home with our own hard earned money. If we're gonna have to pay taxes... at least if we were paying taxes to our own government we would be getting benefits and social services. It's exploitation, pure and simple. —SAWP worker

The history, operation and experiences of workers and challenges to organizing migrant farm workers is covered in detail in Chapter 5 in this book. However, for the purposes of introducing this book on immigrant workers' struggles, the SAWP provides a vivid example of how some of the policy trends and themes discussed so far intersect in concrete terms. The material conditions and struggles of seasonal migrant farm workers in Quebec exist in a global and geohistorical context that includes the ascendancy of neoliberal policies and economic restructuring, the associated international and Canadian trend towards corporatization and industrialization of agriculture and food production in the wake of international competition, and racialized immigration regimes that benefit business interests by providing workers with precarious status and limited rights. At the same time they cohere with official international trade, aid, investment and other economic policies that lead to displacement and increased poverty in labour-exporting countries.

Furthermore, we must also acknowledge a longer-term history of colonization in the Americas that links the migrant farm workers and both locations in which they labour and live. The Quebec — and Canadian — agricultural landbase resulted from genocide, dispossession and displacement of Indigenous Peoples, while the majority of migrant farm workers from Mexico and Guatemala hail from rural Indigenous communities that have resisted and endured marginalization, displacement and many forms of subordination for over five centuries. These communities bear the brunt of the imposition of neoliberal economic policies through international financial institutions and free trade and investment agreements. While millions of small subsistence peasant farmers in Central America have been dislocated in favour of transnational corporations (TNCs) and the reconcentration of land in new corporatized agricultural systems, a few thousand travel north to Canada to work in an increasingly industrialized horticulture production. To cite one pertinent example, 2 percent of the population in Guatemala controls over 70 percent of land. In Guatemala, agriculture provides 60 percent of employment and 22.6 percent of GDP (Krznaric 2005).

Both rural communities in Quebec and migrant-sending countries are withering and disintegrating, after being hollowed out by the restructuring of recent years. This model of "development" is driving farmers off their lands and displacing them, with a lack of local alternative employment. New markets are opened up under structural adjustment programs (SAPs) imposed by the IMF/World Bank and InterAmerican Development Bank, bilateral "aid and development" assistance from official agencies like the United States Agency for International Development (USAID) and the Canadian International Development Agency (CIDA), and a confusing and growing web of the WTO, NAFTA and other regional, subregional and bilateral free trade and investment agreements. Many of these newer agreements go even further in liberalizing the economies than NAFTA and the WTO, not least in areas that impact on agriculture.

The free-trade agenda in agriculture has been set by and for corporate agribusiness. Small farmers all over the world are reeling as tariffs are slashed and subsidies and supports for farmers, if they ever existed, are cut. Meanwhile subsidized corporate U.S. and E.U. farm goods are able to flood local markets and undercut what can be locally produced. The existence of NAFTA has also led to strong resistance against neoliberalism throughout Mexico, while Guatemalan farmers, trade unionists and other social movements have strongly opposed the Central American Free Trade Agreement (CAFTA) with the U.S. Trade liberalization and structural adjustment policies are destroying local productive capacity in rural societies and small farmers' livelihoods. They push countries into cash-crop export production at the expense of domestic food production. With the implementation of NAFTA in 1994, around a million families lost their livelihoods as maize prices plummeted in Mexico due to cheap, subsidized imports. Ottawa is currently attempting to conclude the CA4 (Canada–Central America Four Free Trade Agreement) with Guatemala, El Salvador, Nicaragua and Honduras. The free-market, free-trade and investment model is driving people from struggling small farming communities to seek work far away from their homes and families and, in some cases, in Canada.

Trade liberalization favours a large-scale, industrialized, export-oriented model of agriculture. This is also true of Canada. Under this regime, agriculture has become the arena for a range of corporate integration strategies that seek to control production throughout the food chain and deliver maximum profits. The National Farmers Union, in a paper detailing the context of the crisis for Canadian family farms, describes farms as the "central link in an agri-food chain that reaches from energy, fertilizer, seed, and chemical companies and banks at one end, to processors, packers, retailers and restaurants at the other. Our agri-food chain extends from the oil well to the drive-through window" (2005).

While Canada undermines worker rights in Central America through its trade and investment liberalization agenda, in Canada it maintains a program that fails to prevent exploitation of migrant workers from those countries when they come under the SAWP scheme. Besides its links to neoliberal globalization, the history of migrant labour in Canada must also be viewed in relationship to broader immigration (national and global) contexts.

Thobani (2000) notes that the construction and regulation of migrant workers as temporary and outsiders also contributes to the construction and concretization of Canadian citizens and legitimates their unequal rights and entitlements. Canada also has a history of "unfree" migrant labour — where workers cannot bring families and must return to their country of origin, without rights to regularization. Thobani notes that there is also a legacy of immigrant workers in Canada who have unequal entitlement to social security programs yet must contribute to underwriting the costs of the welfare system. The United Food and Commercial Workers Union (UFCW 2007) highlight the fact that migrant farm workers must pay Employment Insurance (EI) premiums and yet cannot claim benefits. Like Chinese railroad workers before them, this is a modern form of head tax. They help to build the country but cannot stay or have same rights as Canadian workers.

Vulnerability to deportation and lack of legal rights and resources for workers, is exacerbated by the dependency on the employer that is structured into the SAWP. Yet while employers may well hope for a docile, compliant workforce, too afraid to challenge exploitative conditions, intensive farming also brings people together in a space that can potentially be more easily organized than before. Internally, *maquilas* in both Guatemala and Mexico attract many rural workers, but the seasonal worker system creates a form of "floating agricul-tural maquilas" (Justicia4Migrant Workers website). Of course, these have the semblance of being more benign and humane. Yet in terms of actual regulation of the program and the inadequate oversight and accountability of those actors and processes supposed to ensure fair conditions, there are many problems and injustices.

With neoliberal economic restructuring within Canada, throughout the Americas and globally, union/worker rights have come under attack, and migrant workers face new and renewed forms of exploitation in the name of competitiveness and international cooperation (as is particularly evident in the SAWP scheme). As in other sectors, and perhaps more pronouncedly here, the overall trend towards the flexibilization of labour is accompanied by contractu-ally limited temporary/seasonal forms of labour and further privatization of the outsourcing of migrant labour, whereby some Canadian companies directly import their workers with minimal state intervention, as Chapter 5 discusses, and as the expanded Temporary Foreign Worker program is intended to do.

Canada — Current and Future Trends

> Everyone made their money on the immigrant worker — from the big-time capitalist to the slum landlord —— from exploiting his labour, his customs, his culture. He himself had cost the country nothing. He had been paid for by the country of his origin — reared and raised, as capitalist under-development had willed it. (Sivanandan 1982: 103)

Initiatives like the Safe Third Country Agreement and the Security and Prosperity Partnership (SPP) and rhetoric about "Fortress North America" illustrate the way that 9/11 was used to legitimize tighter immigration controls in the name of national security. This trend was already underway. We are witnessing the entrenchment of immigration apartheid, in which a globally (often western-) educated elite are relatively mobile, but the overwhelming majority is temporary, non-status, exploitable and often underground. The immigration points system has become more elitist, while the refugee system provides fewer avenues for appeal. The expansion of temporary worker programs along a more privatized model also expands a class of workers for whom it is more difficult to gain permanent status.

In the 2007 federal budget, the Harper government committed an additional $50.5 million over two years to the Temporary Foreign Worker Program to reduce processing delays, and respond more effectively to regional labour and skill shortages. The twelve occupations chosen for the pilot project include: carpenters, crane operators, hotel/hospitality room attendants, hotel front desk clerks, food/beverage servers, food counter attendants, tour/travel guides, registered nurses, dental technicians, pharmacists, snowboard/ski instructors, and retail sales clerks. According to Human Resources and Social Development

Canada, in 2006 there were 171,844 temporary workers in Canada, a 122 percent increase from ten years ago. Of these, 44.7 percent were in Ontario, 21.8 percent in B.C., 13.5 percent in Alberta and 13.1 percent in Quebec (HRSDC 2006). In September 2007, Ottawa announced a pilot project in B.C. and Alberta to speed up processing times for approving temporary foreign workers in the twelve sectors. The expansion of temporary work programs must be seen in the context of broader immigration policies. These programs are predicated on maintaining qualitatively different sets of rights and status for permanent residents and citizens on the one hand, and temporary workers on the other.

Ottawa routinely invokes increased competition due to economic globalization in its rationale for immigration policy. Canada interacts internationally with other immigrant-receiving countries such as Australia and European nations, including exchanges between policy makers and officials in various forums about best practices for "managing" immigration and related matters (Abu-Laban and Gabriel 2002). The Canadian government has positioned itself internationally as an authority on "immigration management," sharing expertise with other governments, and is an active player in the internationalization of policy, research and information-sharing on approaches to immigration. Such internationalization helps to account for the renewed interest and expansion of guest-worker programs and the overall import and export of policy ideas on regulation of immigration, state multiculturalism and diversity. Further research is needed on the links between trends in official overseas aid and development policy and immigration policy, to examine questions such as the rationale for increased aid for humanitarian resettlement of refugees in order to limit numbers seeking to migrate to Canada.

Conclusion

The prosperity and living standards of people in the North are directly underwritten by the land labour resources of the dispossessed in the South. As a Canadian Labour Congress research report puts it, "The use of labour from the south is part of the transfer of wealth from the south to the north that has been in process since the beginning of colonialism to today" (Cook 2004: 51). The Canadian economy benefits from the triple exploitation of Indigenous Peoples' lands, lives and resources, exploitation of large, "cheap," vulnerable pools of workers in the Third World and the maintenance and expansion of immigration policies and programs that lock many new immigrants and many people from other racialized communities into vulnerable, precarious working and living conditions. At different times, government policy has sought to create, sustain and replenish pools of vulnerable labour through immigration policy. Creating temporary foreign worker programs is one way of doing this, but so too is devaluing the experience and education of new immigrants/permanent residents. Denying them the opportunity to access, acquire or improve English and/or French language skills is another way to achieve this.

The current policy environment emphasizes security, surveillance and control, but leads to heightened precarity for many. Reforms to immigration policy and design are aimed to make Canada more competitive in a global economy. Current developments such as the expansion of the Temporary Foreign Worker Program and the controversial amendments to the *Immigration and Refugee Protection Act* in 2008 under Bill C-50 accentuate and consolidate the trend of the immigration selection process to favour candidates on the basis of ability to contribute to the Canadian economy, treating them as little more than commodities. Moreover, the struggles of immigrant workers in Canada for dignity and justice, which span many years, continue unabated, notwithstanding claims that Canada is an exemplary model of harmony and equality for all. Citizenship and immigration policies are linked to nation-building projects, not only labour and economic policies. Thobani notes that in Canada, "white immigrants have historically been, and continue to be, integrated into the ranks of the 'nation,' while people of colour continue to be marginalized as immigrants, as outsiders to the nation. Therefore, challenging the racialized construction of the nation as bilingual and bicultural is necessary if the processes of racialization are to be transformed in a socially just and progressive manner" (2000: 52). Hope lies not only in addressing this longstanding structural and systemic process, but also with the new forms of immigrant worker organizing that this book explores.

Chapter 3

Making Immigrant Workers

The overall theme of this chapter is the "making of immigrant workers." We draw from the stories of the workers we interviewed to illustrate how the broader political, economic and policy contexts described in the previous chapter shapes the lived experiences of immigrant workers and contributes to creating a category of workers constructed within the current context of international migration. We structured the interviews chronologically beginning by asking people why they left their countries. People leave because they have to: some are seeking a better life but most leave because the situation in their countries is no longer viable. It is a choice within very limited options. We then turn to the experiences of settling, learning about Canadian society and, often for the first time, realizing that their dream about the opportunities in Canada and the reality they experienced were not the same. Finally we looked at work experiences. A large proportion of immigrant workers occupy the bottom of the labour market, in precarious and low-wage jobs where they have little recourse or power.

This chapter presents an overview of work experiences. In subsequent chapters, we discuss the Seasonal Agricultural Worker Program and the Live-In Caregiver Program. We present the interviews in two ways. The first are vignettes or summaries of the story of a particular person or group of people. These will be used to illustrate specific points. The second are direct quotations from the workers themselves. The sections on leaving, settling and working are derived from immigration stories going back thirty years although most are more recent than that. However, these experiences are similar to previous waves of immigration. At the beginning of each section we have selected extracts from the literature that talk about earlier migrations — those occurring at the end of the nineteenth century as well as guest-worker programs in Europe in the 1950–70s. The similarities are striking.

Leaving Stories

We find parallels between the group we interviewed and earlier waves of migration. People leave to seek a better life because of the breakdown of the political and/or economic systems of their counties. As we argued in the previous chapter, these breakdowns are often, and particularly now, tied to the policies and practices — economic and political — of the dominant powers and the introduction of so-called "economic progress." We see this theme repeated in earlier periods of migration. Handlin (1951) attributes the large-scale migration of thirty-five million people from Europe to North America at the end of nineteenth and early twentieth centuries as related to the destruction of traditional rural life, through mechanization of agriculture, which pushed people off the land and pushed the growth of urbanization and migration. He writes:

> The old structure of an old society began to crumble at the opening of
> the modern era. One by one, rude shocks weakened the aged founda-
> tion until some climactic blow suddenly tumbled the whole into ruins.
> The mighty collapse left without homes millions of helpless, bewildered
> people. They were the army of emigrants. (1951: 7)

> Year by year, there were fewer alternatives until the critical day when
> only a single choice remained to be made — to emigrate or to die. Those
> who had the will to make that final decision departed. (1951: 37)

As we discussed in the previous chapter, changes in agriculture have
driven people off the land with few options for work. Even with the export of
manufacturing jobs to developing countries, high levels of unemployment and
urban crowding have led to massive poverty. The restructuring of economies
and agriculture is related to policies of government and to the multiple trade
agreements that loosen any kind of economic regulation. The movement from
poorer to richer countries is directly related to the way that the development of
the former is tied to the latter. This was the case in Europe after World War II
as workers from Southern Europe looked to guest-worker programs as ways to
survive after foreign investment drove their economies into underdevelopment.
Berger and Mohr argue:

> A man's resolution to emigrate needs to be seen within the context of a
> world economic system. Not in order to reinforce a political theory but
> so that what actually happens to him can be given its proper value. That
> economic system is neo-colonialism. Economic theory can show how
> this system, creating under-development, produces the conditions which
> lead to emigration: it can also show why the system needs the special
> labour power which the migrant workers have to sell. (1975: 41)

> An unemployed labour force existed. It existed in a state of underdevel-
> opment, created by the development of those countries now suffering
> a labour shortage. (1975: 126)

In relation to the current period, Mathew comments in his book on organizing
immigrant taxi drivers in New York City:

> We live in a fundamentally divided existence, wherein the life we have
> known for generations has been torn asunder. And yet, at the very
> moment that the familiar social order has been nearly annihilated, the
> possibility of a new one emerges. (2005: 145)

The question, however, is what exactly are the possibilities in their new
worlds? Immigrant workers leave their countries of birth because they feel that
they have little choice, and do so because of hardships brought about by political
and/or economic factors. Many come because of lack of economic possibilities

or because of displacement as a result of war or political repression. Often these factors are tied to the economic interests of more developed countries, or repressive regimes supported by them. Here are some examples from the interviews that explain why people left their countries of origin. One described the economic conditions that he faced, as well as the links with wider global relations:

> Yeah, not only me. Everybody is struggling in the Philippines because of the economic condition of the country; because 60 percent is owned by foreigners, so what will happen to our country, economics? The country will collapse gradually; it's a systematic killing of people down there, the multinationals.

Others talked about the need to flee because of their political beliefs. For example, consider the following notes we made from interviews with three workers from Chile, Lebanon and India:

> Daniel came to Canada in 1976 from Chile where he had been a political prisoner at the time of the overthrow of Allende in 1973. He was forced to leave his family due to the fact that he was always hunted down by the Pinochet regime. He could not get any work because he was "branded" as a political prisoner and leftist.

> Faoud left his wife and four children to come to Canada from Lebanon. His father had been a leader in Fatah. When he died, the organization called on Faoud to join the ranks. He went to the Lebanese authorities for help but was told they didn't concern themselves with Palestinians. He was jailed by Fatah until he agreed to serve. Two months later he got a visa to the U.S., fled there, then made his way to Canada.

> As a university president, Sanjeeve had drivers and servants, but left his comfortable life in his native India after his brother was assassinated for his leftist political beliefs. Warned by the police that his life was also in danger, Sanjeeve lived six months with the constant protection of four bodyguards but the stress of continual surveillance became too much for him: "You have no more personal life." Fearing for his life, he left his wife, son, and career behind to come to Canada.

The push out of their countries has meant that it is impossible to go back and that those leaving have to adapt to what is offered in Canada. As we argued in the previous chapter, the Canadian government is not neutral in constructing the category of immigrant worker, taking advantage of the push from poor countries. It has created policies that draw migrants to Canada to perform cheap labour without any guarantee of permanent status. These programs are designed to fill short-term labour demands in employment areas where other workers in Canada refuse to work. The governments in the countries of origin also benefit from migration: economically they rely on the remittances sent home; as well they succeed in shifting economic and political problems externally. For example, the Philippine government has encouraged mass migration: its economy depends on financial remittances from abroad. The labour export of countries like the Philippines is directly related to the demand for specific labour in countries like Canada, particularly for domestic service work. In addition, the ties of dependence and responsibility with families back home acts to bind workers to low-wage work and to endure difficult work conditions.

Settlement Stories

It is clear from both the empirical research cited earlier and the following interviews that immigrant workers bring education, skills and their hope for better lives to their destination country. However, they then find themselves in a position in which they have to come to grips with new realities and disappointment, all the more difficult because of the high expectations brought on by the myths surrounding the American dream. One of the myths that they encounter is that if they endure dirty work in society, they will eventually achieve social mobility. If they do not achieve this, then certainly their children will be part of the dream; it is a matter of mastering the language and culture of the dominant society. However, this is no longer the reality for immigrants coming to Canada: in today's world they and their children are much more likely to remain on the periphery both economically and socially. They are seen as outsiders. In their work on the German guest-worker programs in the 1950s and 1960s, Berger and Mohr express the shock of arrival as follows:

> The naturalness of his inferior status — the naturalness with which he is accorded his inferiority by people, by institutions, by the everyday etiquette of the metropolis, by ready-made phrases and arguments — would never be so complete and unhesitating if his function and the inferior status which it entailed, were new. He has been here from the beginning. (1975: 113)

When we asked people about their experience of settling in Canada, disappointment and shattered dreams were quickly apparent. Whatever status and skills they brought with them seemed to make little difference here. Further, the conditions they faced were difficult and at times abusive. The following comments illustrate these experiences well:

> Well, the expectations were kind of economic. I thought living here would bring a kind of freedom. When we got here, I was working here and my wife was working here. But I didn't like to see the strong people abusing the weak ones, and I saw a lot of arrogance in the factories. The people had to work hard almost for nothing. And people had no choice but to work in bad conditions because they had responsibilities in their home countries.
>
> Coming from an underdeveloped country, you can see the difference — that here people can buy houses and cars; but the treatment of people is unacceptable. Coming from my country with these kinds of abuses it is somehow more acceptable, but here, where they have human rights, the situation on paper looks good but the reality is different and that is why I get upset.

Funneling people into low-paying work is facilitated by the counselling received from official bodies. Credentials are not recognized: there are major blocks that prevent educated workers from entering the professions of their choice. The belief that any job is better than no job is prevalent. Further, people arriving here feel that there is no choice except to work. This has been explained to us as both the drive to succeed here and as a means, especially for refugee claimants, to get residency. It is important to understand that it is not only the market by itself that structures the position and category of immigrant, but the processes and policies of services provided by government. There is also a not-so-subtle racism about where newcomers are "supposed" to work. We heard stories of trained nurses and hospital administrators from the Philippines who continue to work as domestics, many years after they have arrived. There are many reasons for this, including language barriers and the fact that the demand for re-qualification as a means for recognition involves losing work time and paying tuition.

Another source of pressure on immigrants to stay in Canada and accept poor conditions is the relationship to family in their home country. Remittances from abroad play a significant role in the lives of the families back home and in their country of origin's economy in general. An immigrant worker is often not only working for him/herself but also contributing to the support of relatives and immediate family members in the country of origin. This situation changes the stakes for immigrants in their workplaces: it creates additional pressures to "work hard" and stay employed. Many immigrants willingly accept a drop in social status and live many years apart from their families in order to provide better opportunities for their children. The hope is that their children will benefit from the educational system here in order to achieve some economic upward mobility. This was not the experience of some to whom we spoke, who had come to Canada with some schooling. Immigration meant that their prior education was not recognized, forcing them to repeat all or part of secondary school.

> Imagine you already graduated [from high school] and here you have to start all over again....

Our interviewees indicated that the settling process is one in which immigrants begin to see the realities they face in Canada, including the lack of decent job prospects and the lack of real support from government. This leads to reduced expectations and at times, a growing awareness of the social and economic forces that that keep them in jobs at the bottom of the labour market.

We include the following vignette, summarizing in more detail the life of one person, to illustrate the process of de-valuing new arrivals. We have chosen this interview because it clearly illustrates the drop in status, the lack of long-term prospects and the complicit role of government and community agencies in this process.

Ahmed

Ahmed (thirty-nine years old) came to Canada from Algeria where he was a biologist and ecologist *par excellence*. He was considered an expert in his field and was a regular commentator on radio and other media. His wife was employed in the Algerian department of fisheries. They gave it all up to come to Canada in pursuit of a more peaceful country.

With his professional background he was easily accepted as an immigrant within Canada's point system, but that didn't mean employment reflecting his training and experience would be easy to come by. Ahmed began by looking for jobs that he felt he was qualified for. "I was even ready to leave Montreal to work as an oceanographer. I applied all over the place. I never even got a single call back."

"The employment agent, she must make $50 per hour. Do you know what she told me? She said, you want to work as an oceanographer? Well, you should go to such and such an address in the Old Port. I got there, they were looking for ship captains — she couldn't even take the time to find out what oceanographer meant — either that, or she took me for a fool."

The agent steered Ahmed towards a community organization that provides immigrant services, where he followed a three-week course in job-search training. "They told us that we shouldn't devalue ourselves, that we should valorize our skills and experience, that we should ask for payment that reflects our worth. I learned very quickly that that is not the way it works here.... If I had followed their advice I never would have gotten a job.... I took bachelor off my c.v. — you have to understand employers want to save money — they won't recognize an immigrant's qualifications and they don't want to pay you for it."

"I followed a ten-month intensive *Attestation d'études collegial* — an equivalency course for immigrants that qualifies you to work as a lab technician... there were people with masters and doctoral degrees in chemistry in the class... we learned basic chemistry and biology that qualified us to do what you can do with a high school education." The course promised to place graduates in jobs in a variety of technical fields with good pay. "That was false advertising." They did nothing for Ahmed in terms of finding work, much to his frustration. "I learned through experience.... You have to go door to door to every company."

Ahmed knows he is not the only over-qualified immigrant with trouble finding work. "All the immigrants that I know, they're in the same situation." With all the qualifications the government demands of immigrants, he figures it must be this way to protect Quebec's own educational system and graduates. "I think it's there to protect the universities, otherwise they would all go out of business." Ahmed finally found a job as a lab technician. He works the night shift from 11 p.m. to 7 a.m. "No one else there has as much training as I do, they all have Secondaire 5." From the quality of his work and the leadership he demonstrated in the lab, his employers eventually caught on that Ahmed had more training than he had indicated. Though they now recognize his qualifications, that doesn't translate into more official responsibilities or higher pay, nor does Ahmed demand either of those. After two years of unemployment, he is just happy to have a found a job. "You need a lot of courage and faith to get through unemployment — to live unemployed in Montreal is so hard."

One of the ways that immigrant workers were able to counter some of these difficulties was through the creation of community. Some had a contact, a friend or family member, who was already here. This person encouraged them to follow and paved the road for them. The building of social connections, therefore, begins even before leaving and becomes the first step in setting up networks of support. Ahmed, for example, worked as a volunteer in a collective community garden: he became involved in the organization that established these gardens. For others, such as Filipino women, the church was important. These places are important because they create opportunities to meet people from the country of origin or others from the local community.

Work Stories

Work is central to the lives of new arrivals, not only because people need income to survive and to be able to send money home, but also because it is the test of how they succeed in their new country. Many with insecure immigration status, such as refugee claimants or those in the Live-In Caregiver Program, need to work in order to improve their chances of securing permanent residency. From a historical perspective, immigrants have been used as a pool of cheap labour. One could argue that, without the demand for cheap labour, there would be far fewer immigrants allowed into Canada. The connection between migration and cheap labour is a universal phenomenon. Handlin (1951) talks about the immigrants from Europe to North America at around the beginning of the twentieth century: their experience of the labour market has important parallels with the contemporary period. In particular, migrants are vulnerable to abuse with little recourse.

> These elements of insecurity, the immigrant learned, were not confined to the conditions of the working day; they pervaded a total relationship of the worker to the economy. The fluid labor supply that gave the employer complete liberty to hire as many workers as he wished, also gave him the ability at will to dismiss those whose toil he no longer needed. (1951: 74)

The work stories that we were told confirmed what the literature said about the place of immigrant workers. Despite education and skills, they end up in low-paying and precarious jobs. All of those we interviewed had relatively high expectations of Canada. While they expected to live through a certain period of transition, they also expected that they would be able to find work that reflected their qualifications. Instead they found themselves filling positions at the very bottom of the Canadian labour market. The experiences of Filipino women in the LCP and Mexicans in SAWP will be discussed in Chapters 5 and 6.

People feel that there is no choice but to accept what is offered. The new labour market, characterized by sub-contracting, requires people who are desperate. As one of us noted in talking to an Indian worker:

> Sanjeeve learned very quickly that jobs reflecting his qualifications were impossible to get. He found a couple of temp jobs thanks to friends. In both cases, workers were not hired directly by the employer but rather by an agency, who kept close to half the wages of the workers they "contracted" to factories and farms. One job was in a factory making ice cream. The workers were all people of colour — from different communities. The only white people in the place were the supervisors. Standing up for your rights was out of the question. "Talk about your rights and the next day you're not there!"

One of the Latin Americans we interviewed, who had been in Canada longer, had settled into more stable employment, but also experienced barriers and limited mobility, or was offered jobs that did not match his level of education. As we note in the extract below from notes taken during an interview with him, he is very aware of the clear division between those born here and immigrants.

> He studied in a CEGEP (Quebec college system) and began his career as an information analyst. He has been working in this field after completing his CEGEP technical studies in Montreal. He was working for the Ville de Montréal for a couple of years but actually has not been able to hold stable employment. He works by contract. He believes that it is because of racism. He states: "Many times, even though you know the French language, it is forbidden to work here in some places. You are not allowed to be admitted because you were not born here. Some places, like the Ville de Montréal, where there is a lot of work to be done, but you are not allowed to be part of that status quo because you are an immigrant… There are places that it is actually impossible to work."

The jobs offered to immigrants presented major challenges. Face-to-face conflictual encounters with employers and supervisors were common, along with situations of feeling marginalized because of being part of a racialized minority group or because of their vulnerable status as new immigrants. Experiences of racism were frequent. One of the most striking features of the interviews is the type of supervision and discipline described. It was generally arbitrary and always direct: workers had little or no autonomy in their jobs. The conflict in the workplace then manifested itself as direct, face-to-face conflict with supervisors. As one worker we interviewed recounted,

> I remember a long time ago, a woman was coming from Afghanistan; and after a few weeks, she started wearing something on her head. The other co-workers were complaining about it, the manager tried to get rid of her but not directly. You know the supervisors never really like it when people take time on Fridays to pray or something; in the beginning, they say nothing because they need the people but after a few months, they start to ask them for those Fridays, they don't really respect their religion.

Many faced situations in which they were vulnerable to pressures from employers, even in violation of their right to unionize. In the quote below we see divide-and-rule tactics. One woman said:

> There was a woman who wanted to make a union, and the boss started pushing her around. This woman had been sitting next to me and then the boss came and asked me if I would be a witness saying that it was her that had caused it; and I said, "Never in my life! He tried to bribe me, but I said, no way, you can't buy me!"

Others felt pressures of arbitrariness and pressures to increase production. This theme has been repeated many times when people come to the Immigrant Workers Centre. Usually older women face this kind of pressure. The production in textiles or apparel is subject to restructuring, "just-in-time" production and shifting ownership by companies, which in turn creates instability and greater pressure on workers. One woman told us the following:

> Then they sold it [the company that employed her] to [a company] and they were nice at first. The wages increased, and at first they discussed things with the workers and they respected the seniority of workers. But later on they changed their strategies. I noticed that people were starting to be laid off. People with seniority were beginning to be laid off. That was my observation. [Later through a different company]: Yes, they abused our working hours, they were permanently dismissing people with seniority. They did it by asking 100 percent efficiency from people who were already very old.

Despite the fact that there is legislation to create minimum labour standards, the working conditions in jobs described to us were often in violation of these standards. For domestic workers this is common. We will develop this further in Chapter 5, but here is one example of a woman who had to endure long hours despite the fact that these long hours contravened labour standards:

> It didn't work well. I just worked with them for about two months and one week. Well, the female employer was always complaining about my work, she wasn't satisfied… And it was always long hours. The contract was supposed to be fifty-one hours, but I always worked fifty-five to sixty hours a week, without getting paid overtime. But it was supposed to be overtime after fifty-one hours."

We use the concept of "learning in reverse" to describe the process of becoming an immigrant worker. This concept refers to learning to accept and accommodate to the harsh economic conditions and lack of possibilities for improvement. The immigrants we spoke with all have had to learn to navigate the doublespeak of the Canadian immigration system, which recruits highly educated and skilled people to fill the very bottom of the labour market. Immigrants must learn to "unlearn" their status — to deny their social status and education, to hide their "over-qualifications" and adapt to this bottom of the labour market. One worker expressed this contradiction very succinctly:

> I followed a ten-month intensive Attestation d'études collégiales [college equivalency course for immigrants] that qualifies you to work as a lab techni-

cian… There were people with master's and doctoral degrees in chemistry in the class… We learned basic chemistry and biology that qualified us to do what you can do with a high school education.

Another aspect of this deskilling process is using the skills people have while not recognizing their accreditation. This allows employers to benefit from the higher level of training but not compensate the worker. For example, domestic workers often have been trained as nurses. In their jobs they provide a high level of care but are paid as domestics. Thus, regardless of training and background, it becomes very difficult to attain proper status.

Those without formal status are the most invisible of immigrants to Canada. They have no rights and can make no claims to the regulatory bodies that, in theory, are supposed to limit the degree of exploitation in the labour market. The following vignette describes the experience of one person we interviewed who remained in Canada although his refugee claim was refused. He decided that returning home brought too many risks.

Since he arrived here close to five years ago Omar has been working under the table. He has worked in a variety of jobs in the service sector: in bakeries, with fresh produce, in distribution, as a bus boy, as a cook and in factories. His being "illegal" makes working difficult. He doesn't stay in a job for too long, out of fear that he will be recognized and discovered by authorities. As a result he moves from job to job. He has lost track of the number of jobs he has had.

Fear of discovery is not the only reason he changes jobs periodically. Like other illegal workers here in Quebec, he feels he must put up with working conditions that other workers do not. His capacity to stand up for his rights is limited. He knows that he has no security and that he has only a support network of friends to rely on — as do his employers. Employers know they can pay him less, give him less hours and tell him to do a variety of difficult and menial tasks. He has no choice, other than to move on to another job.

Conclusion: Becoming an Immigrant Worker

Hope for? What do I have to hope for? In this life you only have so many years to make a contribution, to do something with your life. Those years have been robbed of me. The only thing that I have to hope for is that no one has to go through what I am going through.

This chapter summarizes some of the experiences of immigrant workers in Canada. We have seen that people leave their countries because they feel there is little choice and that the changes in their countries that push people out are often linked to a world economy dominated by the capitalist corporations and interests emanating from North America, Japan and Europe. The process of economic and social restructuring always causes displacement: many who have some skills and education decide to take the risk and leave. Countries of origin export not only highly skilled and educated people, but also those whose means of subsistence has been shattered by processes often referred to as "economic development." Another economic process involved with migration is that of remittance: monies sent home by migrants play an important role in both the welfare of families left behind and in the general economy of those countries of origin. Interviewees told us that even though they left their countries of origin for various reasons, they still have strong personal and familial ties to their home countries, as well as a financial responsibility to those left behind. The pressure on immigrants to find and maintain jobs is increased by this relationship.

The current wave of immigration occurred in the context of a restructuring of advanced capitalist economies. The consequences included the increase in service work, precarious and low-wage employment and jobs that have been difficult to unionize. Even though many new arrivals come with high levels of education, this does not translate into "good" jobs. The contradiction that is so often expressed is that Canada is looking for qualified immigrants, but the reality is that the qualifications count for little. Immigrant workers have little power to negotiate the conditions of their labour. The relations learned in the workplace, such as arbitrary power relations, lack of stability, poverty, long hours and lack of respect, shape the construction of the category of immigrant worker. People accept this at least partially because the ties that bind include remittances to family members and escape from repression. Learning to adapt to desperate situations is another aspect of immigrant or refugee life. This was particularly vivid for those awaiting government decisions about their refugee claims or their status. The combination of all of these realities creates a category of immigrant workers that is used in this particular context to respond to the demands of the particular conditions of the labour market. In our analysis the intersection of race, class and gender are critical in understanding how it is that the category of immigrant worker is constructed in the contemporary period. People arriving in this wave of immigration are for the most part "people of colour" who are slotted into the jobs we have discussed. We have seen this phenomenon as part of the legacy of the immigration policy of the government of Canada. Gender is key as well: the most striking example of this, discussed in Chapter 6, is the Live-In Caregiver Program. Domestic work is considered to be women's work: it can be imported as cheaply as possible. Both gender and race are clearly present in the experiences of the workers we interviewed.

Class is more complex. Mandel (2004), drawing on his analysis of interviews with Eastern European workers, argues that class has both "objective" and "subjective" factors: these include how the society is structured, the place people occupy based on their position in the division of labour and how people internalize and act on this knowledge. Objectively, immigrant labourers are part of the working class: economically, they are at the bottom of it. The interviews we conducted tell us that workers feel this disappointment, but have begun to accept their marginalized position. In other words, they gradually learn to let go of initial high hopes and expectations and begin a process of learning in reverse. How this translates into action will be discussed in Chapter 7. We quote Hart at length as she captures the essence of the intersection of race, gender and class for immigrant workers:

> The ideal worker becomes a self-sufficient nomad, migrating with moving job possibilities, keeping specific ties to neighbourhoods, friends and families suspended long enough not to interfere with the need for mobility.... People who are unwilling to move because they rely on established social networks rather than risking both unemployment and social support do not display rigidity, inflexibility, "fear of change"... as much as a realistic assessment of actual chances for survival. (Hart 1992: 88–89)
>
> In sum, the new *generic worker* must be able to adjust to indeterminate change, and is characterized by low expectations regarding pay, work conditions, and above all job security... new jobs will not be enough for workers to get by, but will have to be combined with other employment... as well as work associated with unpaid social and personal services. In short, the new workers will be "working like women" whose flexible working patterns have already made them into preferred labour force in many instances. (Hart 1992: 88–89)

The immigrant worker is ideal as this "generic worker." Immigrant workers have arrived in a situation in which their choices are restricted. They have often come from situations of desperation, leaving their home countries as refugees or because of economic hardship. They also carry responsibilities for families at home. Some resist, but many accept, that their dreams of what Canada might offer are just that — dreams. Adapting to the realities can mean reducing expectations and just surviving with what the job has to offer. "Learning in reverse" refers to the experience of "loss," of letting go, giving away, being stripped of some value, some identity and social status, which was formerly "me," and now is not. The daily life of immigrant workers requires that their learning is how to survive, to live with disappointment, low incomes and instability. The challenge is to learn to "work hard and stay employed" no matter how bad the jobs, and to keep your expectations low in order to take what is offered. Part of becoming an immigrant worker is to unlearn a former status and identity: the immigrant learns to "re-define the self" as "updatable resource," not "human being." This process is about learning to navigate the doublespeak of public life, to fear the bosses, to be silent about your rights and recognizing that possibilities for action are limited. At the same time that immigrants learn that injustice exists, they can learn to resist it by taking action and by demanding respect as human beings.

Chapter 4

Access to Social Rights for Migrants to Canada

The Long Divide between the Law and the Real World

Canadian and Quebec researchers have documented the policy and social barriers faced by migrants trying to access health and social services. They range from limited eligibility for programs, to systemic barriers within the health and social service network, to socio-economic and cultural factors of discrimination (Oxman-Martinez et al. 2005; Baines and Sharma 2002; Zaman 2004; Pierre 2005). Issues of gender and immigration status have been shown to be of particular importance in understanding the barriers to health and social well-being (Preibisch 2007; Guruge and Khanlou 2004).

Many international conventions, as well as federal and provincial legislation such as the *Canada Health Act* promise universal access to health care and social services. Most notably, the Convention on the Protection of the Rights of All Migrant Workers and Members of their Families (CPRMWMF), in force since July 2003, enshrines human rights protections specifically for migrant workers (though Canada is not a signatory). The International Covenant on Economic, Social and Cultural Rights (ICESC) recognizes "the right of everyone to the enjoyment of the highest attainable standard of mental and physical health." Yet despite the official rhetoric, research in Canada indicates that migrants do not benefit from equitable access to social rights. For instance, when accessing the health care system, research has shown a significant proportion of migrants to Canada experience delays, complications or denial of medically necessary treatment (Caulford and Vali 2006). This is particularly true of those with "precarious immigration status" — that is, those who are denied the permanent right to remain in Canada and/or whose status depends on a third party such as a spouse or employer (Hanley and Shragge forthcoming).

For migrants to Canada, barriers to health services are influenced by legal, institutional, socio-economic and cultural factors. Linguistic barriers often prevent or complicate communication and action (Gibson et al. 2005; Kopec et al. 2001; Zanchetta and Poureslami 2006). Also, migrants to Canada report cultural barriers in accessing public services, such as a lack of understanding of ethnic-specific norms (Lai and Chau 2007; Stephenson 1995). Such issues are likely exacerbated for those with precarious immigration status, for whom barriers to social rights are often systemic. The exclusion of temporary workers and recent immigrants from health services for the initial three months of their residency impedes equitable access to health care (Oxman-Martinez et al. 2005). Also, health costs and loss of wages due to work-related injury may not be compensable or compensated due to provincial workers' compensation restrictions, which lead to the de facto exclusion of many migrants (Lippel 2006; Preibisch 2007). Such policies are compounded by bureaucratic barriers, such as misfiling or miscommunication, which increase delays in receiving social benefits or even result in unjust refusals (Gravel, Boucheron and Kane 2003).

Our interviews with migrant workers revealed that respondents had repeated struggles in trying to access social programs and benefits. The experiences of the migrants we encountered highlight the many barriers they face in accessing their social rights, whether legal, socio-economic and cultural. In this chapter, we share their stories in three areas. We begin by presenting the difficulties respondents faced in accessing a range of social rights including labour standards, unionization, Employment Insurance, workers' compensation, health services, education, recognition of foreign training and basic human rights. Next, we turn to a discussion of the themes related to barriers in access that respondents identified, the most important being fears related to immigration status, racial and ethnic discrimination, economic barriers, access to legal representation and cultural barriers.

Migrant Access to Rights

Among the more than fifty migrants with whom we spoke, many shared stories of challenges they faced accessing their social rights. Labour-related issues were a common preoccupation (probably in part because that was the basis on which we approached them). Education and recognition of foreign credentials were common themes as well. Here, we present some of their experiences.

Labour Standards

Under the law, any employee (with very few exceptions) is covered by the province's minimum labour standards. These standards cover such things as minimum wage, overtime pay, vacation time, sick leave and dismissals. In theory, all workers should be given the same treatment. As we hear from Amado, however, violations are common, and, while the Labour Standards Commission is often helpful, this is not always the case:

> Well, like other Filipinos, they expect like Canada is heaven. But when I came down here, "Oh my God!" All of the companies I've worked at in Canada, I've complained with the labour standards!… Yes, the labour office was really helpful. I never went to the office personally, I just called them by phone…. But sometimes I think they are in collaboration with the factories. — Amado

Even when people do have a union, they do not always receive the support they need to fight the violation of their rights. We have seen examples of collective agreements from immigrant workplaces that were below the minimum standards, and, in Maria-May's story, the union actually told her not to complain:

> I made my complaint at the Normes de travail [Labour Standards Commission] with the help of the IWC. The union discouraged me and said it would not

> make a difference. I won my case because I was not given eight weeks notice [of my layoff], and I received compensation. — Maria-May

However, despite these difficulties, many — like Amado and Maria-May — stepped forward to defend their rights anyway.

Workers' Compensation

Similar to Labour Standards, workers' compensation is meant to cover all employees; however migrants with unclear status are often excluded. Domestic workers (overwhelmingly immigrant and female) are explicitly excluded in the province of Quebec, amongst some other provinces. In the case of work-related illness or injury, workers are meant to receive compensation and medical remedy. Research shows that immigrants who do make workers' compensation claims have low rates of acceptance (Gravel et al. 2003), and our interviews indicate that many are not even aware that they can make such a claim:

> After four years in the job, the emission from the plastic fumes irritated my eyes to the point of forcing me to quit work. I did not receive CSST or unemployment benefits, mostly because I didn't think I would be eligible. — Maria-May

Employment Insurance

Forgive us if we are starting to sound like a broken record, but the situation for Employment Insurance is similar. In theory, anyone who pays into EI should be able to claim benefits if they have enough hours and are laid off, ill or need to care for a sick family member. As this migrant farm worker explains, though, temporary workers regularly pay into the EI fund without ever being able to claim:

> Every year they take off this unemployment insurance but we see none of it — I've been here eighteen years working and I've never touched that money… Imagine — it's a disgrace! — Julio

Temporary workers' immigration status comes into question when they lose their job, since their presence in Canada is tied to the employer specified on their work permit. Until they have a new employer-specific work permit, they cannot work legally. EI officers sometimes trap them in a catch-22 by saying that they are "not available for work" until they have a new work permit and are therefore not eligible for EI.

Another problem is that the conditions imposed by EI sometimes prevent people from taking the necessary steps to improve their employment prospects. Rather, it is structured to get them to return to the same type of work, as quickly as possible:

> When I was laid off, I applied to EI but after six months Human Resources told me I had to stop going to school or we will cut you off. So I made negotiations with the school and told them that I didn't want to be cut off and that leaving

was temporary. Then I went down to the immigration office and said, "When I first came down to Canada, you told me to go to school, and now Human Resources is telling me to stop." — Amado

Labour Code and Unionization

Migrants are under-represented among union members in Canada; however, having a union was seen by most respondents as helpful, providing a sense of security in the workplace and someone to go to if they needed information or support:

> Well, the union was comforting, I guess. Because when you're in trouble, you need people to tell you how things work, that one and one is two. She [the union representative] was very supportive, she explained to me where I could go to get help and because I have a union, the union is supposed to take care of it. You know, I always walk with this book [my collective agreement], everywhere I go. — Juvy

Unfortunately, however, many perceived the laws surrounding unions to be weak:

> Quebec labour laws... What can I say? The labour laws we have in our countries are much better than here. In our country if you organize a union, the company will not close. The labour laws are exploiting and repressive to the workers. But the policies [in the collective agreements] themselves... Like, for an increase, ten cents a year! But sometimes it will be frozen! You know how it goes. Another thing is that if you join a union in a company here and the management knows, they will kick your ass. — Amado

Fears of unionization leading to job loss, whether due to factory closings or repression, are not unfounded:

> Others are afraid [of being associated with the union] because the manager knows who is part of the union and they are afraid that they might lose their jobs... Also, when you have a union, you always have to go through them [and can't use the Labour Standards Commission]. It limits me to a certain number of rights. — Lida

Education

All children residing in Quebec, regardless of immigration status, are meant to have access to free, public education. The children of tourists are excluded from this access, but in principle, the children of undocumented residents are meant to be included. Registering for school, however, can be a major challenge for the children of undocumented parents. School registration requires the presentation of identity documents from both parents and children: as well, they are expected to prove their legal residency in the province. This is most commonly done by showing the Quebec health card, a card that temporary residents may not possess and which is definitely not held by undocumented residents. Neighbourhoods with a high number of migrants are used to this situation and their school officials will generally enroll children, but parents are often wary of declaring themselves to a public authority. A further complication is that there is no clear funding arrangement to cover the education of undocumented children.

One challenge in children's education that is particular to Quebec is that all non-Canadian new residents are required to enroll in French language schools. This has been a policy that has done much in terms of preserving French as the public language of Quebec, but it is often unexpected and resented by migrant children who previously studied in English. Nadine, a youth sponsored to come to Canada by her LCP worker mother, expressed frustration with this system. When she arrived in Montreal, she was placed in a "welcoming class," a program for newly arrived immigrants to learn French and integrate into the Quebec school system. In Nadine's experience,

> Immigrants are forced to learn French. You're not allowed to speak your language; you're not allowed to speak English. I didn't like how they forced you to.

Frustration with this system is reported to be one of the major reasons explaining the disproportionate rate of school drop-outs among Filipino youth, many of whom are sponsored by their LCP mothers (Pratt 2003).

In terms of adult education, all temporary residents are required to pay foreign student fees to attend publicly funded institutions — a requirement that puts studying out of reach for most. In addition, a student visa is required if they plan to take more than a few courses and a student visa cannot be held at the same time as another type of visa. For those with full access to education at Canadian rates, however, socio-economic factors block many migrants from furthering their education or upgrading their skills. Getting time off work, giving up employment income, family responsibilities and the length of time one may have been away from studies were all mentioned as barriers to migrants taking up courses. One interview respondent's age made him feel out of place:

> Frankly speaking, going to school is not appropriate for my age. I am taking an English course. It is not easy to get the education for my age.

It is necessary for migrants to Quebec to speak French in order to access quality employment and other opportunities; but it is not easy, especially for those who expected to do well in Canada with their well-developed English skills. In a similar vein, migrants who arrive with excellent knowledge of French, common for example among North and West African migrants, are bitterly disappointed to be thwarted by their lack of knowledge of English. This need to be bilingual in Canada's two official languages is a layer of complexity unique to the Montreal context.

Recognition of Foreign Credentials

Given that migrants to Canada are often selected according to their professional and technical qualifications, the lack of recognition of these qualifications and their past job experience is a source of anger for many once they arrive in Canada. A foreign-trained blacksmith explained to us:

> I quickly found out that your qualifications from outside are not recognized… you are forced to accept menial jobs.

In most cases, migrants to Canada enjoyed a certain degree of status, educational and financial privilege in their home countries. Otherwise, the prospect of migrating to Canada would have been impossible due to the cost of applying, the requirements of our selection system and the cost of travel. The difficulties encountered in the Canadian job market are a major disappointment and play heavily on people's self-esteem:

> Immigration does not instantly mean that you will have work. First you must study; there are things that frustrate you. You feel mediocre because the things you have studied in your country do not level up to the standards here.
> —Linda

Settlement agencies and immigration authorities encourage people to seek equivalency recognition from professional orders and from Canadian universities, but foreign qualifications are systematically undervalued. Many migrants are at first open to the process but soon find it overwhelming:

> Then one wants to dedicate himself to his profession. But here there are no such opportunities. One must begin from scratch, to study once again, go back to school because we do not have the same level of education in out Latin-American universities. —Emilio

The need to work, support family members in Canada and send remittances home to family are further factors impeding people's return to education and training.

Socio-Economic Barriers to Social Rights

While the previous section outlined the ways in which migrant workers are often excluded from access to the social rights which many people born in Canada take for granted, this section explores the barriers that make such access difficult. Insecurity related to immigration status, fear of deportation and lack of Canadian experience are barriers exclusive to migrant workers. Most other barriers identified by respondents, such as knowledge of rights, racial and ethnic discrimination, language, economic status and poor legal representation, are factors shared to varying degrees by Canadian-born people of colour, women and the poor.

Immigration Status and Fear

As discussed in our introductory chapter, migrants to Canada arrive with a range of immigration statuses that confer differing degrees of security in terms of the right to stay in Canada. For those with temporary statuses (temporary workers, refugee claimants and, especially, the undocumented) the threat of deportation is real and Canada's supposed commitment to the protection of human rights is no guarantee of safety. One refused refugee fighting deportation told us:

> I feel it is outrageous and unacceptable that Canada would endanger [my] life and well-being… by deporting [me] to the end result of [my] ending up in Egypt, while maintaining a claim that Canada does not deport people to torture. — Yasser

For permanent residents, the threat of deportation is less imminent (in theory possible only under circumstances of serious criminal activity or fraud in the initial application); yet many immigrants reported a fear of losing their jobs or rocking the boat by demanding their rights. Because the ability to continue supporting their families was paramount, they expressed a constant underlying concern that they might lose their immigration status or that their actions might imperil the eventual granting of Canadian citizenship.

As a consequence of this basic employment insecurity and the high competition for jobs, migrant workers feel that they can be easily replaced. This feeling greatly lessens their confidence in handling challenging work conditions:

> I do not think someone will help me if I take some actions to challenge my working conditions. For immigrants, it is so, so hard to get a job. Although it is a labour job, I care about it. If I quit, somebody else will do it. — Saloua

In several interviews, people talked about giving up the expectation that they will be treated equally with Canadian-born workers:

> Most of my colleagues [local people] are not satisfied with the condition. They always complain about the low salary and busy schedule. In fact their salaries are much higher than mine. But I do not want to compare with them, because I am a new comer. I do not want to lose my job. — Frank

Even worse, the competitive context of insecurity can lead to distrust among the workers. When asked about the dynamic between workers, about whether they spoke with their colleagues about their labour rights, seasonal farm workers told us:

> We have to be careful because there are people, ones among us workers, who will tell the farmer. He tells the consulate and it's over for us.

The fear of not being called back for subsequent contracts and losing access to the Canadian labour market is pervasive.

Lack of Canadian Employment Experience

Our interviews revealed that one important reason for the higher rate of unemployment among qualified immigrants is due to what Canadian employers call "lack of Canadian work experience." Many immigrants face years of frustration, trapped in a vicious circle as they try to find a job that will give them their first "Canadian work experience" in their field. Even though many migrants have several years of work experience in their home country, they need to be prepared to start with a blank c.v. in Canada because their work experience is often worth nothing here.

> When I arrived here I looked for work in computer science. There was simply none because I did not have documents to show since [as a refugee] I could not leave [Chile] with official documents. On the other hand, I did not have experience. It was spoken of as Canadian experience and because I did not have any, it was a vicious cycle. I presented myself from one side to another, and they kept saying to me that I must have a minimum Canadian experience of six months. I could never obtain it. — Patricia

This barrier was not just limited to professional jobs.

> Even for a labour job, you have to compete with lots of people who have the "Canada working experience." — Lamine

Knowledge of Rights

Migrants' knowledge of their rights was a major theme that was brought up by the people to whom we spoke. People had mixed feelings about the usefulness of knowing what their rights are in Canada. For Maria-May, for example, she felt that her employer harassed with HR (human resources) notices specifically because she had knowledge of her rights. Another worker reported that he had no knowledge of his legal rights as a Canadian labourer and had no real interest in learning about them. He is cynical about his political power as an immigrant to Canada:

> I am weak. All the immigrants are weak. It is not our world. How can we challenge? — Chen

For those who were among the only ones in their workplaces with knowledge of their rights, the situation wasn't easy. Nadine describes her second job at a plating factory where the conditions were very poor:

> It was the most dreadful work I've done. I was there about two years. It was really tough. My hands were bleeding; we were standing for half the day. We could only sit after lunch… We'd complain, but we had no choice — we had to work. My other co-workers, they have families — they didn't speak French, they had difficulties in English. We complained, but we stayed.

Nadine, like most of her co-workers, felt that her options were limited. She needed the money, had a limited understanding of what her rights as a worker were and hadn't gained the confidence to assert herself in the Quebec context. In her workplace, this created a situation where workers were unwilling to challenge their bosses.

When newcomers' lack of familiarity with the local context was combined with a low level of education, the situation was even more difficult:

> The others didn't want to join [the union]. I told you, most of the employees over there didn't know anything and they just know how to sign their signature... They have only Grade 3 or 4 education. They are old too. One was fourteen years old when she started working there so they hadn't studied at all. They know how to speak but they don't know how to write. — Rudy

For those who did know about their rights, we asked them where they got this knowledge. For most, the learning occurred in discussions with other migrant workers and, in some cases, with Canadian-born colleagues. Some of our interview participants had come across government information pamphlets, and others had sought support and information from community groups such as the Immigrant Workers' Centre. For some of those with whom we spoke, the concern with rights preceded their arrival in Canada, and was sometimes the very reason they were forced to migrate in the first place (as in the case of political refugees). For these workers, it was second nature to seek out knowledge of their rights.

Racial and Ethnic Discrimination

Racial and ethnic discrimination was felt by most of the people we interviewed. Even when they had been here a long time, the feeling of exclusion from the mainstream often remained strong:

> After all these years, I don't really feel that I'm a Quebecer, because of the colour, because of the accent... but we are Quebecers. We are Quebecers for the referendum, for the elections, for the income taxes... but in the practice, you never quite fit. — Enrique

This discrimination doesn't fit with the image people had of Canada before arriving. Several told us that they had chosen Canada as a destination precisely because they had heard that there was minimal discrimination in Canada. One respondent said,

> What disappoints me a little bit is the discrimination. I thought Canada is an immigrant country and immigrants will be treated equally. But my experience told me discrimination is everywhere.

Some interview participants felt that racism was getting worse in Canada. They saw it as prevalent among private citizens, employers and institutional representatives:

> When I came to Canada at first, I never used to see Black people too much. So then now you see so much Black people. Maybe the White people begin to feel threatened. I saw this RCMP officer on T.V. and he was talking about prejudice among the RCMP. Before when you would see a police, you could get in the car and he would take you where you wanted to go. Now you stop the police and he thinks you want to kill him or something, like jumping out with a gun! So things change now. Now I think they are more prejudiced so now you have to withdraw yourself from a lot of people. — Lida

Although people work around it, racial and ethnic discrimination was felt to limit people's possibilities, as expressed by this migrant:

> I would have liked to help immigrants further but I feel blocked by the fact that I am a Black immigrant woman and a single parent. — Licia

Language Barriers

Not surprisingly, the challenge of learning or honing French and English language skills was a major concern for the migrants with whom we spoke. It was identified as a major barrier to their being able to exercise their full rights: it was also seen as a basis for discrimination. When migrants first arrived in Canada, they told us that the demands of just settling in made it very difficult to concentrate on language, an even harder task in the bilingual context of Montreal:

> It was so hard to learn English for me, after my arrival in Canada. People only spoke French, which was so hard too. When one leaves his country it is so hard to learn anything in the first years. — Marco

This sentiment was shared by others:

> Montreal is international metropolitan with two kinds of cultures. Bilingualism is a must for most of the time. I knew nothing about French before I came here. Now I can speak Chinese, English and some French. So becoming multilingual is a big adjustment for me. — Xin

English-French bilingualism was just the tip of the iceberg for workers trying to integrate into a diverse employment setting. Trying to understand and defend labour rights in this context is extremely difficult:

> Well, at the very beginning, when I was witnessing this kind of injustice, I couldn't do anything, because there is this transition period when you are dealing with people from different nationalities. I was trying my best to learn French and communicate with them but some people speak Portuguese, Italian, and it was hard. Often the supervisor would try to impose their language on other people. It was hard to communicate in French. — Enrique

The complexity of the language situation in Montreal leads many migrants, especially those whose English skills were already strong, to consider leaving Montreal for other Canadian provinces or the United States. French speakers are sometimes drawn to Quebec's smaller cities (Sherbrooke, Quebec City, Trois-Rivières) in order to escape the need for English.

Insecure Employment and Economic Situation

The changing nature of work, with a trend toward short-term, temporary, contractual work, is a phenomenon with negative effects for all Canadian workers. Migrants are particularly caught up in this dynamic. Many of those we interviewed felt very uncertain about their future job prospects. A farm worker, when asked if he would return to work in Canada the following year, said,

> [I will] come back if I can, if the boss requests for me to come back. No one knows if the farmer will ask us back.

In such a context, solidarity between workers — let alone between different ethnic communities on a shop floor — is next to impossible. For many of those we interviewed, the precarity of the job put standing up for your rights out of the question:

> Talk about your rights and the next day you're not there! — Rajesh

In a related vein, one worker told us that, although his employer now recognizes his qualifications (previously, they benefited from his skills without giving any recognition), that doesn't translate into more official responsibilities or higher pay, nor does he demand either of those rights:

> I could never ask that. Never. Never. Things are very competitive. If I demand that, I'll lose my job and I'll be on the street and I can't do that. That'll be on my record and I'll never get another job. — Ahmed

After two years of unemployment, he was just happy to have a found a job. This working mother described a similar imperative:

> Our economic situation was very bad, with the need to stay home from work because my children were ill, but at the same time the necessity was go to find any work because we had not sufficient money. — Pata

Legal Representation

In some cases, the cumulative impact of all these barriers led migrants to seek out legal services in order to exercise their rights. However, the high cost of legal representation and the uneven diligence and honesty of lawyers was a problem reported by several participants. The immigration councillors and lawyers Rajesh encountered were, in his view, lying opportunists who encouraged him to exaggerate and falsify his story: for example, they told him to change his name and say that he was Sikh, in order to win his refugee case more easily.

Conclusion

The academic literature affirms that there is a clash between Canada's official rhetoric about the country's reliance upon immigration as a nation-builder versus the ways that migrants are excluded from a range of social rights. Critics such as Rodriguez (2002) argue that it is not only a matter of a disjuncture between what Canada purports to uphold and the actual reality for immigrants in terms of health care and other social rights; it's also a question of the assumptions made about rights and claiming rights in a (capitalist) system, which, as a fundamental aspect of the way it functions, explicitly denies/undermines those rights to many people. The discussions we had with migrant workers confirmed these trends. Migrants often choose Canada expecting equal treatment: they are bitterly disappointed with their actual experience.

Migrants have trouble accessing labour, education, health and other rights due to explicit policy exclusions (often differing according to immigration status), and due to institutional practices and socio-structural barriers. Individual actions play a role in these exclusions, but the bulk of the weight is institutional and systemic.

Chapter 5

Seasonal Agricultural Workers

"They treat us like slaves! The Mexican government sells us and the Canadian government exploits us." That's what Ejidio (a pseudonym) has to say about the Seasonal Agricultural Workers Program (SAWP). In existence since 1966, the SAWP has grown exponentially in the past decade, providing the pool of cheap indentured labour needed for agribusiness to take hold and expand. Through the SAWP, Mexican and Caribbean migrants work on farms in Canada for up to eight months a year. They are housed on-site, earn slightly above minimum wage, pay into Employment Insurance (EI) and the Canada Pension Plan, and, in theory, enjoy the same rights as Canadian workers.

The Canadian government holds the SAWP up as a model. The program allows the agricultural industry to fill labour shortages, while workers avoid the risks associated with illegal migration, while earning more than they could in their home countries.[1] For international bodies such as the World Bank, International Labour Organization and the U.N.'s Global Forum on Migration and Development, temporary labour migration programs are key components of an emerging neoliberal model of migration and development. In this model, immigration, which comes with theoretical legal protections and citizenship rights, is being replaced by state-structured labour mobility programs, or temporary migration — with workers dependent on their employer for legal status: some of these organizations are also advocating the possibility that remittances replace international aid as a key strategy to ensure "development" of countries in the global South (Gibb 2007; Global Forum on Migration and Development 2007; International Labour Organization 2002).

A critique of the SAWP, which has been in existence for forty years, has been well-established by workers, labour and human rights activists, researchers, NGOs and unions. Yet, while media attention and public awareness are growing, the current Conservative government's immigration policy is eroding the few protections which the SAWP ensures workers. This year's passage of bill C-50 increased temporary migration through the Temporary Foreign Worker Program (TFWP), formalizing a trend well underway in Quebec agriculture since 2003. Temporary foreign workers now make up close to half of the migrant agricultural labour force in the province, with many employers taking advantage of the greater flexibility of the TFWP (in comparison with the SAWP) to erode work conditions and undermine current labour organizing efforts.

Most scholarship, research and advocacy work on the SAWP has focused on Ontario, where 80 percent of temporary workers in Canada are placed (Preibisch 2007). Our study augments this already rich critique, while focusing on the material situation and struggles of migrant agricultural workers here in Quebec, locating the SAWP and TFWP within an analysis of neoliberal transformations in agriculture and in immigration policy, and while exploring worker resistance, through a profile of the organizing work of the United Food and Commercial Workers Union (UFCW)-supported Centre d'appui aux travailleurs et travailleures agricoles migrants.

With strong roots in the Filipino and South Asian communities of Montreal's Côte-des-Neiges neighbourhood, the Immigrant Workers' Centre (IWC) has worked primarily with immigrants and refugee claimants working in low-paid industrial and service-sector jobs, as well as with women employed under the Live-In Caregiver Program (see Chapter 6 in this book). Yet it is impossible to ignore the situation of migrant agricultural workers labouring only a few hours away in rural Quebec to feed consumers in the city. With temporary foreign worker programs undergoing expansion, the struggles of these workers for justice and dignity are increasingly important. For this reason, the IWC and the Centre d'appui have been making an effort to collaborate in recent years: sharing information, supporting each other's campaigns and coordinating efforts to pressure governments to improve policies related to temporary migrant workers.

Of the roughly fifty immigrant workers interviewed as part of the broader research leading to this book, six of these were labour organizers connected to the Centre d'appui, and seven were workers with some relationship to the Centre (five Mexican men recruited through the SAWP and two Guatemalan men recruited through the TFWP). We ground our analysis in their stories, which bear many similarities to those of urban immigrant workers we met during this project. Workers employed across sectors and with varying immigration statuses have described to us the push factors driving them from their home countries, their family responsibilities and the importance of remittances that bind them to their jobs, and the vulnerability that forces them to put up with working conditions few Canadians would find acceptable. What distinguishes the SAWP and TFWP, as we will see, is the workers' extreme vulnerability and isolation that are structured into the programs — a precarity created by, condoned and actively coordinated by the Canadian state.

This chapter begins with an overview of neoliberal transformations in agriculture (both domestically and across North America) and immigration policy in Canada. In doing so it highlights parallels between the current neoliberal conjuncture and earlier phases of colonialism. This is followed by a critical presentation of the SAWP and TFWP. We then present a case study of the Centre d'appui, contextualized by the UFCW's efforts to unionize migrant farm workers across Canada. Quotes from the seven workers and six Centre d'appui organizers we interviewed are interspersed throughout the chapter. All names have been changed with the exception of Patricia Perez, founder the Centre d'appui, who passed away in October of 2007. This chapter is dedicated to her memory.

An organic farmer I know has a poster in his barn that dates back to the 1940s. It depicts two farmers working their field while watching over their shoulders as a group of factory workers whistle off to work, lunch boxes in hand. The caption reads: "And if we worked 40 hours a week, what would you eat!!??" City people have a tendency to romanticize agriculture. Farming is hard, dirty, dangerous work, and it is a sector that has been virtually untouched by the labour movement gains of the past two generations. In that time, workers have fought for the right to bargain collectively, for minimum employment standards, workers' compensation, health and safety rights. However, as progressive legislation was passed, the agricultural sector argued successfully that small, family-farming operations occupied a distinctive niche in the economy and should be exempt from these reforms. Farm workers are exempt from labour standards legislation in most provinces (Labour Codes in Canada fall under provincial legislation, and the application of a patchwork of labour standards varies from province to province); in Quebec and Ontario, they are denied the right to unionize. Actual union rates for agricultural workers in Canada are less than 2 percent (Cook 2004).

The popular logic that justified agriculture's exemption from labour-rights legislation is that farming somehow exists outside the capitalist system — it is a family affair and would never survive the increase in production costs associated with improved working conditions. This was among the arguments used by employers to counter recent unionizing efforts in Quebec. It is true that times are tough on Canadian farms, but the portrait of the farmer who relies on his family and neighbours to help bring in the harvest no longer reflects reality for the vast majority of agriculture operations in Canada.

The last two generations have seen massive transformations in Canadian agriculture, with sharp drops in the number of farms and increases in the size of farms. The trend has intensified in the past two decades: the number of commercial farms increased 26 percent during the 1990s, and the number of very large farms doubled (Preibisch 2007a). There have been similar transformations further along the production chain. Four companies dominate the food retail sector in Canada, a market share that gives them considerable power in terms of structuring farm production (NFU 2005).

An important exception to this trend is the organic sector, where direct marketing schemes such as community supported agriculture and farmers' markets are creating an expanding niche that allows producers to escape the pressures of the dominant agricultural market. But, for the most part, the farmers who have survived have bigger fields to tend, fierce global markets in which to compete, tighter production budgets — and a harder and harder time finding local people willing to do the work.

The introduction to this book describes in detail how, in the current period of neoliberal restructuring, Canada's immigration and economic policy work together to create a new underclass of immigrant workers. Domestically, neoliberal economic policy drives down working conditions for jobs at the bottom of the labour market; while the immigration system creates a pool of precarious labour, desperate enough to fill those positions. Internationally, Canada is an aggressive proponent of agricultural trade liberalization, a process that is displacing millions in the global South, while attracting the newly displaced through guest-worker programs like the TFWP, SAWP and the Live-In Caregiver Program (see Chapter

6 in this volume). That poverty levels for newly arrived immigrants are more than three times those of other Canadians (Tran and Chu 2006) is not the result of our social order dancing to silent music conducted by the invisible hand of the market. The state holds the marionette sticks, and immigration policies are the strings. The case of migrant agricultural workers is a stark example, where the restricted rights associated with their immigration status, along with the vulnerability and isolation imposed by the terms of their work contract, creates an explicitly racialized labour underclass.

This symbiosis between economic and immigration policy is not a new phenomenon. Sunera Thobani (2000, 2007) argues that Canada is a colonial creation established on lands stolen from Indigenous Peoples and that it has always been a racialized state built by — but not for — immigrants of colour. Historically, citizenship rights have been withheld from various groups, defining the terms upon which they were integrated into the economy and effectively creating an underclass of workers of colour. This is most classically illustrated by the experiences of Chinese immigrants who built the railways, yet battled the head tax and exclusion acts to win citizenship rights. The Canadian tradition of relying on a racialized underclass also has firm roots in agriculture. In British Columbia, the Punjabi community has long provided the workforce for horticulture while battling systemic racism (Patwardhan and Monrow 1982; Fairley et al. 2008). In Quebec, the provincial farmer's union, l'Union des Producteurs Agricoles, has coordinated programs to bus workers (over 95 percent of whom are new immigrants and refugees) from Montreal and other urban centres to local farms since the late 1970s (Mimeault and Simard 1999).[2]

The SAWP — a temporary migration program with no possibility for participants to apply for permanent residence or citizenship rights — emerged in the late 1960s, at a time when immigration policy in Canada was supposedly liberalizing. Yet the following comments of Susanna, a Centre d'appui organizer, underline the racism that continues to inform immigration policy, in an albeit less overt fashion:

> There was a racist intention behind the entire creation of the program: they saw a Black labour force entering the country and they wanted to find a way to prevent them from integrating into the population at large. The program dates back forty years but the spirit remains the same.

She goes on:

> Agriculture is the hardest work and the worst paid and has the worst conditions — but it's easy work to get. So people stay in it five, eight years, but then their kids don't stay in the sector... So how do you solve that problem? With a program like this one where workers are confined to the agriculture sector, and their kids don't come, and you don't have to see them in banks and hospitals. At first the government's argument was we don't give them residency because we don't know if we'll need them next year — it's a seasonal need that varies from year to year. But the labour shortage isn't temporary and it isn't

unpredictable. Every year they bring in more workers, and they're working almost year round now. We sent a letter to a minister asking, "Why don't you give them residency if you know you'll need them next year?" It's a question of discrimination. The response was — they didn't realize what they were saying — they said: "If we gave them residency they wouldn't be obligated to stay in the agriculture sector." So it has nothing to do with a temporary need. It's "you stay in agriculture and you stay there."

That the Canadian state is engineering a racialized underclass through programs like the SAWP is not a new phenomenon. What is unique to this current period of neoliberal restructuring is the way our economic policy and supposedly colour-blind immigration system function together, to radically intensify the poverty and precarity of new immigrants within Canada, while coordinating and organizing their movement on a global scale. Emblematic of this trend in neoliberal immigration policy is the rapid expansion of temporary labour mobility programs, for which the SAWP is an important predecessor, providing an international labour outsourcing strategy for a horticultural sector that itself has been massively transformed by neoliberal restructuring over the past decades.

With the signing of the North American Free Trade Agreement (NAFTA) in 1994, Mexican markets were opened to imports of subsidized U.S. corn — the markets were soon flooded. Imports more than tripled in the ten years following the agreement, driving corn prices down by half (thanks to government subsidies, U.S. corn is sold well below the cost of production), disrupting traditional agriculture and forcing more than 1.5 million small farmers off the land (Ackerman et al. 2003; Wise 2007). Both NAFTA and the structural adjustment policies imposed on Mexico after the 1982 peso crisis stipulated the dismantling of rural support programs for campesino agriculture, enforcing a model of cash-crop, export-oriented production at the expense of domestic food production and rural development (Patel 2007). According to Sandra Polaski of the Carnegie Endowment for International Peace, "The rural poor have born the brunt of adjustment of NAFTA" (2006: 1). The rural poor either end up working on new export-oriented corporate farms that are replacing campesino agriculture, or they head north to the *maquiladora* assembly plants in the north of the country, or across the border into the U.S. and Canada as migrant workers.

Free trade and investment have brought about a related process of consolidation in Canadian agriculture. The Canada-U.S. Free Trade Agreement of 1989 and NAFTA made way for increased integration of Canadian with U.S. and Mexican markets. Trade and investment liberalization favoured large-scale, export-oriented production. At the same time, NAFTA and other bilateral trade deals are intensifying competition in both U.S. and Canadian markets, as trade barriers on agricultural imports from Mexico and Central America are removed (Brem 2006). In the words of Stan Raper of the UFCW,

The agricultural industry in the last 20 years has completely changed. Historically small family farms dominated the agricultural sector, but the motto for farmers right now is go big or stay home — and corporate farming and factory farming have taken over the landscape. (2007)

In 1996, 5.5 percent of horticultural farms produced 42 percent of the fruit and vegetables grown in Canada (Weston and de Masellis 2003). The industry has expanded and consolidated considerably in the past decade.

Competition among agriculture operations is only part of the squeeze being exerted on farmers. The National Farmers Union describes farming as "the central link in an agri-food chain that reaches from energy, fertilizer, seed, and chemical companies and banks at one end, to processors, packers, retailers, and restaurants at the other" (Brem 2006). They note that in Canada, as elsewhere, each link in that chain is now dominated by a small handful of multinational corporations, 76 percent of which are posting record profits while farmers have been in the red, scoring below depression-level earnings in fifteen out of the last twenty years. In the labour-intensive horticulture sector, farmers have been reduced to lower-middle managers in this corporate agri-food chain — with serious implications for workers' rights. A necessary ingredient for the consolidation of agribusiness in horticulture is a large pool of workers, precarious enough to accept the degraded working conditions offered in this emerging sector.[3] Big farms require a big pool of just-in-time workers: the SAWP fills the gap.

The SAWP began as a pilot program between Canada and Jamaica in 1966, in response to farmer demands to address labour shortages on Canadian farms. the SAWP was expanded in 1967 to include English-speaking Caribbean countries[4] and Mexico in 1974. The program has grown steadily over the past two decades, in step with the expansion of, and consolidation in, the agri-business sector (Preibisch 2007a, 2007b). Since 2002, employer groups have been able to recruit beyond countries participating in the SAWP via the Low-Skill Pilot Project (LSPP) under the TFWP, a strategy used widely by employers in Quebec who are relying increasingly on Guatemalan workers recruited through the LSPP. Over 22,000 SAWP and TFWP workers came to Canada in 2007: they were assigned to farms in every province, with the exception of Newfoundland. Roughly 80 percent end up in Ontario, home to more than half the horticultural industry in the country, where over 1600 growers depend on the program. In Quebec in 2007, 500 growers employed close to 5000 temporary foreign workers.

The SAWP and TFWP are managed in partnership between the Canadian government and the agricultural industry, represented by the Foreign Agricultural Resource Management Service (FARMS) in Ontario and the Fondation des Entreprises en Recrutement de Main-d'oeuvre agricole Étrangère (the Foundation of Companies for the Recruitment of Foreign Agricultural Labour) (FERME) in Quebec. In the case of the SAWP, bilateral agreements between Canada and sending countries are formalized in a memorandum of understanding laying out the terms and conditions of employment and detailing operating guidelines from worker recruitment to repatriation. Employment contracts are negotiated trilaterally — between FARMS or FERME, Human Resources and Social Development Canada, and sending-country governments. Temporary work permits are issued by Citizenship and Immigration Canada; recruitment is done through labour ministries in the sending countries. The modalities of the TFWP vary somewhat from those of the SAWP, the most significant difference being the reduced level of government regulation. The TFWP does not require bilateral agreements with sending countries, allowing employers to deal directly with labour-recruiting agencies.

The popular logic underpinning such guest-worker programs is that labour shortages are short-term and temporary. Statistics suggest otherwise. The number of migrant agricultural workers in Quebec has increased 30 percent over the past two years. Workers are in the province year-round, from January 1st to December 15th (followed by the two-week absence stipulated by the terms of the program): they do everything from greenhouse work to Christmas tree production (Brem 2006). Preibisch (2007a) notes that in central Canada, foreign workers are replacing the domestic agricultural workforce: the program has thus become a crucial, institutionalized component of the horticultural industry. In 2000, SAWP workers made up 53 percent of the workforce in the sectors where they were employed (Brem 2006); their presence has increased by close to 50 percent since that time (Preibisch 2007b).

The agricultural industry often argues that without the SAWP to fill labour shortages, horticulture would shut down. What is less acknowledged in popular discourse is that without the SAWP, corporate agriculture in central Canada could never have taken shape — at least not in its present form. Ontario's horticulture industry expanded 90 percent from 1994–2000 (FARMS 2003). In the 1990s, the area devoted to greenhouse production more than doubled (Weston 2007), as did revenues, which in 2003 stood at $2.1 billion (Purdy 2005). Canada has become a net exporter in six of the seven crops in which SAWP workers are concentrated (Weston and Scarpa de Masellis 2003). Leamington, Ontario, has become Canada's "Tomato Capital," boasting the highest concentration of greenhouse production in North America (Ferrier 2006; Preibisch 2007): the Mexican consulate has opened an office to provide services to the SAWP workers who make up the majority of the local workforce. Only a program on the scale of the SAWP could have provided a pool of just-in-time labour large enough for agribusiness to expand and precarious enough to accept the conditions offered in that emerging sector.

> We're the ones the boss gives the hardest work to. The Canadians won't really put up with that much hard work, so that means we're left with all the dirty work — with the sun, the rain, the cold — because we're working continuously. There are probably people here who say we're getting rich — but it's the opposite: we're making you all rich. — Victor, a migrant agricultural worker

A quantitative portrait of migrant farm labour in Quebec agriculture is difficult to paint; FERME does not publish statistics on the sectors in which SAWP and TFWP workers are present, nor does it reveal the size of the farms in which the workers are placed. However, growth in the horticulture industry and in the number of SAWP and TFWP workers suggests a similar trend as that found in Ontario.

> You have to concentrate. Better if you don't think about time — that's how you can deal with working until seven at night. At first the rows just seem to get longer and longer, and I would look at them and say to myself: "God, how am I going to finish this?" The first days it was hard but after, you learn not to look up. You keep your head down. But if I get up every now and then and look and see how much farther there is to go, I lose hope. I wonder how the hell we're going to finish all the work that's left. So I just focus and look down and think about my family. — Lorenzo, a migrant agricultural worker

Ejidio has spent eight months a year working on Canadian farms for the past twenty years, yet he is no closer to qualifying for residency status or claiming the EI benefits he's been paying into than the first day he arrived. A typical workday starts at dawn. He's in the field applying pesticides or harvesting furiously to keep up with the tractor he has to load until six or seven — often without a break. Then it is back to his shared camper to shower, cook dinner and get some sleep. The living conditions are crowded and substandard, he resents his boss and is outraged by the deductions that the Canadian government takes off his paycheque. There's an atmosphere of fear among his co-workers — they know that if they stand up to the boss, they risk getting sent home fast.

> The chemicals they use are really strong. One time they were spraying the greens and the very next day we had to go out and harvest them! Look at my hands — they're covered in blisters. If one of us gets dirt sprayed in his eyes, they hardly bring us water to rinse it out with. The other day they sent another one of us back to Mexico. He got sick and they couldn't cure him so they sent him home. That's not right — it's not justice! — Ejidio, a migrant agricultural worker

The fear felt by workers like Ejidio is contextualized by the power imbalance structured into the SAWP. According to the SAWP contract (HRSDC 2008: 6), employers have the power to repatriate workers for "non-compliance, refusal to work, or any other sufficient reason." This has included refusing unsafe work, falling ill and questioning wages (Brem 2006). In most cases, according to the Centre d'appui, the order comes within twenty-four hours and the worker pays their ticket home. The Centre estimates a few dozen workers are repatriated every year, but it is hard to specify exact numbers. In many cases, workers are coerced to sign documents stating they are choosing to break the contract: FERME will not release statistics on repatriations.

The SAWP sets up an indentured relationship, with workers dependent on their boss for housing, transportation and, most crucially, their immigration status. This leaves them isolated and vulnerable: it makes challenging their boss very difficult. The program stipulates that workers must be housed on-site. Their movement, visitors, mail and phone calls are often monitored, and in some cases

---

Fraisebec

Fraisebec, one of the largest strawberry producers in Quebec, attracted media attention in the summer of 2007 when it was revealed that the sixty Guatemalan women
workers housed on site were not allowed to leave the premises, nor receive visitors.
The advocacy-oriented Centre d'appui aux travailleurs et travailleuses agricoles (CATTA)
has documented two reported suicide attempts among the workers (CATTA 2004).
Serious concerns about the working and living conditions on the farm have attracted
the attention of Amnesty International as well as the Quebec Women's Federation.
Quebec's Human Rights Commission has opened an investigation.

---

controlled. Most employers in Quebec retain workers' documents — including
their health cards. "Lack of basic freedoms is a big problem," explains one of the
Centre d'appui staff. "Some workers have spent more time here than in Mexico
for the last twenty years; and they can't decide when they go to the doctor, who
they have the right to see, or when they can get a drink of water."

Employers can ban workers from the program; they can also "name," or
request the return of, workers with whom they are satisfied. Roughly 80 percent
of SAWP workers are hired through this naming process. Another organizer at
the Centre d'appui explains:

> It gives bosses the ultimate word. Workers have no opportunity to defend
> themselves. The boss can just not like someone and say they're alcoholic, even
> if they've never drunk in their lives. In one case a worker was accused of being
> a "leader." What's that!!? In another the boss said they were a bad worker but
> the worker said, "No, he just doesn't like me because we had a conflict."

Risking their chances of being "named," or called back, and the threat of
arbitrary repatriation makes workers scared to speak out; but intimidation is not
the only factor that keeps them silent. In 2006 a Centre d'appui organizer told us:

> Workers feel and act as though they are non-status workers, despite the fact
> that they are here as part of a legal program. They are afraid to stand up for
> their rights — most have absolutely no idea what their rights are as workers
> in Canada.

Minimal efforts are made by the government departments coordinating the
program to inform participants of their rights; it is primarily thanks to groups
like the Centre d'appui that they get that information. As one SAWP worker
described:

> Because of Daniel and Maria [CATTA organizers], Mexican, Guatemalan and
> Salvadoran workers know the laws. Before, I didn't know them; our bosses
> never gave us that information — they totally used us. They would tell us what
> to do and we would be blind, we would just do anything. We didn't really have
> rights. They would lock us up, they wouldn't tell you anything, just threaten to
> put you on a plane to Mexico, and that was fine for them because we didn't
> know the laws. Now I just thank God that I'm learning about the laws.

Another worker told us:

> So now I've learned what the laws are. There are laws that protect workers against discrimination. Now when we mention that, the Quebecois listen to us. Now I know. I can say to the boss "Would you do that to a Quebecois? Would you treat them that way?"

But even armed with knowledge of their rights, the repatriation clause undermines workers' ability to make demands — and without effective mechanisms to enforce the rules that exist on paper, investigate infractions or mediate disputes, the safeguards that do exist are ineffectual. Susanna, another organizer at the Centre d'appui, put it well:

> Before, most workers didn't know their rights. Now most of them know their rights but they don't demand them — not because they don't know them, but because they can't. "Yeah, I know I have the right, but what do you want me to do? What? You want me to demand that from my boss? What do you think he'll say?"

In theory, consulate staff are supposed to defend workers' interests, but the structure of the SAWP and TFWP places them in substantial conflicts of interest. Consulates compete for placements; if one consulate deems housing on a given farm to be substandard, the consulate from another country can accept those conditions and, in so doing, secure a long-term relationship with that particular grower. Competition is fierce. Since 2003, all newly created jobs have gone to Guatemalan TFWs. These now make up close to 50 percent of the temporary migrant agricultural workforce. Given the importance of remittances to southern economies, it is easy to imagine the reticence of consulate officials to make demands on Canadian employers or the government. Remittances are second only to oil in terms of contributions to Mexico's GDP: they are therefore considered a pivotal factor in development strategy (Hernàndez-Coss 2005).

An anecdote shared by a Centre d'appui organizer reveals the consulate's negligence and the stakes involved for workers:

> One of the first farms on the program, they hire lots of Guatemalans, Indigenous campesinos who don't talk Spanish, so they're super vulnerable. When they first arrive they're told only half will stay the season. They work fourteen hours a day. One worker called us — he couldn't walk anymore. He wanted to go home to Guatemala. He called the consulate and he was told that "No, you can't go home." He couldn't walk anymore. So he told them, "I can't work anymore — it hurts too much" and the consulate told him, "You have to, or else you pay the whole ticket home." He said, "I want to leave, I want to pay it and they won't let me." — Susanna, a Centre d'appui organizer

One worker, who had contacted the Mexican consulate when his boss refused to take him to the doctor said, "I told the consulate, he told me to shut up or they wouldn't get new placements." Another worker commented on the attitude of the consulate, saying: "The consulate is supposed to defend us but really it's the consulate and the bosses that help each other." Indeed, the priorities of the Mexican consulate can be inferred by examining the resources it devotes to supporting SAWP workers. A staff of three is responsible for the roughly 3000 Mexicans employed in Quebec. Operating hours of 10 a.m. to 3 p.m. is a complete mismatch with the schedule of workers, who are in the fields from dawn to dusk. Presumably workers are meant to leave a message at the consulate, which would then call their employers in order to contact them.

The SAWP and the LSPP share the dubious distinction of being the only migration programs in Canada that offer no possibility of claiming eventual citizenship status (because of workers' low occupational classification, they can never qualify as permanent residents). This places workers, especially those who have been coming to Canada for years, if not decades, in a kind of limbo — paying taxes to a government that does not represent them and contributions to social programs like EI for which they do not qualify. Estimates of SAWP contributions to the EI fund are well over $11 million (Cook 2004). It is a bitter irony that is not lost on the workers we spoke with. As one worker put it,

> They look down on us; but the Quebecers, when they finish their contract, the government pays them all winter long. But us, who pays us all winter? We have to pay our own bills at home with our own hard-earned money. If we're going to have to pay taxes — at least if we were paying taxes to our own government we would be getting benefits and social services. It's exploitation, pure and simple.

Another, describing the lack of support for workers and their families in their home countries, said,

> We pay all this insurance money and we go back to Mexico and once we get there we need to find a way to pay for the medical treatment. We need to get over what working here does to our bodies. There should be a hospital set up back home to deal with all the sickness and injuries that we have when we get back there from here. There should be some kind of program or benefits so that our families can be taken care of — so they'll get medical coverage there too. Here, they take all this money off our paycheques but we don't get any benefits and there's zero social support for our families.

Another worker, in his eighteenth season in Canada, had this to say:

> Every year we lose our jobs. We return to Mexico and live like we're unemployed. We receive absolutely no benefits, no extra money. Now I'm claiming a pension — I'm going to get seventy-one dollars a month. That's an insult. I'm not going to find work anymore. I have three small children to support — one is seven, another is four — on seventy-one dollars a month!? I've been coming since 1973. I just turned sixty-three. What benefits will my family receive? What will they have gotten out of these eighteen years? I've spent so many years coming here and they never once told me about this pension I'm entitled

> to. And if I hadn't asked for it, they would never have told me — they would never have given it to me.

It is perhaps unsurprising then that 25 percent of Mexican workers in Ontario surveyed by the North-South Institute reported being treated poorly by their employers (Brem 2006). The tales of abuse and assault surfacing in the Quebec media are shocking. The Centre d'appui has documented many cases of substandard and overcrowded housing, with no indoor plumbing or hot water, long hours with no breaks or available drinking water, verbal abuse, threats and violent assault, and dangerous exposure to chemicals and pesticides without proper training or protection. Such abuses point to another fundamental flaw in the SAWP: workers have no formal representation, no voice in contract negotiations and no recognized group defending their interests. No formal appeal body exists to resolve disputes. The need for worker representation is made more acute by the strong voice and powers that employer organizations enjoy.

Administration of the SAWP was effectively privatized in 1987 and transferred from HRSDC to FARMS, a consortium of agribusiness representatives that now coordinates the program in Ontario. FERME was created in 1989 to coordinate the SAWP in Quebec. FARMS and FERME are not publicly accountable. Their boards of directors are appointed from the commodity groups participating in the SAWP and TWF. Their budgets come from the user fees charged to growers participating in the program. Through FARMS and FERME, agribusiness consortiums not only administer the SAWP and TWFP, but also play a major role in setting immigration policy direction through contract negotiations and program evaluation (Brem 2006). Given the growing importance of the temporary migrant worker programs, this amounts to a de facto privatization of immigration policy.

A strong critique of the SAWP and TFWP has emerged from faith-based groups, human rights organizations, activist groups such as Justicia4Migrant Workers, as well as large unions, including the UFCW (United Food and Commercial Workers), the B.C. Federation of Labour, Alberta Federation of Labour and the Canadian Labour Congress. Their demands to government include provisions in the programs for workers to apply for citizenship, tighter enforcement of the safeguards that exist on paper and an independent third party to mediate disputes. However, the government has made no effort to strengthen and enforce existing safeguards; instead, these are being undermined by increased use of the newly expanded Temporary Foreign Worker Program, a program used to hire not only agricultural workers, but also workers in hotels, hospitals, the tar sands, fast food restaurants, construction, meat packing and other sectors.

It would appear that Canada does not have a problem with "labour short-ages," but rather a problem finding enough workers who will accept the degraded working conditions being offered in sectors taking advantage of the TFWP. The Alberta Federation of Labour, in its analysis of the promotion of these temporary worker programs, suggests that, "At least some employers are using the program as part of a deliberate effort to drive down wages and working conditions and to bypass unionized Canadian workers" (AFL 2006: 1). The union notes that, "in a sense, the program is being used as a union busting tool. And, by allowing the program to be used in this way, our provincial and federal governments are allowing themselves to become partners in union busting" (AFL 2006: 1).

> Here in Canada, well, no one wants to do the work that we do. When they put Quebecers to work doing what we do in the fields, they only last a couple of hours at a time. I've never seen one that came in at six or seven in the morning and worked alongside us until six at night. — Mauricio, a migrant agricultural worker

This is certainly the case in Quebec agriculture, where use of the TFWP is undermining the already minimal protections afforded SAWP workers and busting the unionizing efforts underway. In 2003, FERME initiated a pilot project via the TFWP to bring Guatemalan workers to Quebec farms. In five years the program has mushroomed from 215 workers in 2003 to 2255 in 2007 (Guatemala 2008): this figure now represents almost half the temporary migrant farm workforce. Meanwhile, Mexican placements have stagnated at around 3000 (Morin 2007). The popular explanation for the shift is that, as Mexican workers have begun demanding better conditions, farmers are seeking a new source of more docile workers. This is most definitely the opinion of one Mexican SAWP worker whom we interviewed:

> They see that the Mexicans are showing their claws and want to defend their rights, so now they prefer the Guatemalans because they are more silent... they are threatened in their country because, before they enter this program, they're asked many questions. They're frightened, intimidated. If the landlord doesn't name them back, they don't come back to Canada. We have to teach them their rights. All farm workers here in Canada, from around the world — we all need to fight for our rights.

Now these workers have also begun organizing, so in a stated attempt to subvert the union campaign, employers are looking to Colombia and Central America to recruit workers. "If there are workers that don't like the conditions here, they can go find work elsewhere — it's a big world," FERME director René Mantha told *La Presse* in the summer of 2007 (Morin 2007).

> I'm not scared. I don't care — if the boss doesn't ask me back, or if the secretariat doesn't let me back, it doesn't matter. I just don't want the workers who come after me to have to go through what I've had to go through. — migrant agricultural worker participating in the UFCW union drive

The summer of 2008 marked a historic victory. Workers at Mayfair Farms in Portage la Prairie, Manitoba, ratified the first-ever contract to cover migrant agriculture workers employed seasonally at a farm in Canada. Ninety-three percent voted for the three-year contract, which includes a grievance procedure, the right to be recalled seasonally, based on seniority, and protection from eviction or repatriation until their case is heard by an independent arbitrator.

Such a breakthrough has been harder to achieve in other provinces. In Ontario, the UFCW has had to turn to the courts, challenging provincial legislation that barred agricultural workers from joining unions. The case went all the way to the Supreme Court of Canada, whose 2001 *Dunmore v. Ontario* ruling found that the province's Labour Code had violated the Charter of Rights and Freedoms by infringing on workers' freedom of association. Ontario has yet to change its Labour Code to conform to the ruling. There, agricultural workers have been granted the right to join or form an association but are still barred from collective bargaining.

There is a similar story here in Quebec. In June 2006, 150 workers on three farms voted to join the UFCW and submitted a request for union accreditation to the Commission des Relations du travail du Quebec, the provincial labour relations commission (LRC). Their employers and FERME challenged the request, arguing that the Quebec Labour Code does not apply to migrant workers because they are not Canadian citizens. The LRC rejected these claims and accredited one of the three union requests to a group of workers employed in a year-round greenhouse operation. But the LRC denied the request of workers at the other two farms, citing a clause in the Labour Code that prohibits unionizing on farms that employ less than three workers year-round (according to the terms of the SAWP, migrant workers are only allowed in Canada from January 1st to December 15th). As discussed earlier, the logic underpinning the legislation is that small "family" farmers exist, in a sense, outside the standard capitalist economy and that the increased costs associated with improved working conditions would bankrupt growers. That some of the province's largest horticultural producers acted as spokespeople during the media campaign reveals the fallacy involved in making such claims today.

The unionizing campaign was nevertheless an important breakthrough, bringing the situation of migrant agricultural workers into public debate. This was the result of long years of organizing, and Hector was a large part of those efforts. With eight seasons working on farms in Ontario and Quebec, Hector is a kind of veteran of the SAWP: after five years of contact with the Centre d'appui, he knows his rights and played a pivotal role in organizing workers on his farm. "All we ask is that they respect us," he told us in an interview in 2007. "People ask me if I am scared doing this work, and I say no! I didn't kill or rob anyone. All we are asking for is that our rights be respected. If I get fired, if they send me back to Mexico, they will know they have to respect us, as human beings."

Hector's courage is admirable considering the battles he has fought. He was fired soon after union accreditation was filed, because his boss learned of his organizing work. "He stopped me while I was working which was around 5 p.m. and told me we were going to the airport at 1 a.m. next morning," he recalls. With the support of the Centre d'appui, he successfully challenged the dismissal: "In the hearing, the farmer said that he would pay me for the hours that were stipulated in the contract, that he would give me all my documents back and that he would pay for my airplane ticket — and that I would return to work for him."

Organizing efforts in Quebec began in 2003, thanks to Patricia Perez, a Mexican woman who originally came to Montreal as a political refugee. She began visiting SAWP workers after she received a desperate phone call from a worker who had gotten her number from the cousin of a friend. "I was shocked," she recalled during an interview in 2006. "He didn't even know where he was." The man's employer had stopped paying him after a workplace injury left him unable to work: the employer refused to bring him to see a doctor. The worker was repatriated following Patricia's first visit; the Mexican consulate refused to answer her questions. "So that's how I started going out every week. The second time I went into the field, there were fifty workers waiting to talk to me and the farmer shoved me out." The following year, when the UFCW offered to fund Patricia's support work, the Centre d'appui was born. Now in its fifth year, the Centre has a paid staff of three and has just secured its first storefront office in St-Rémi, an agricultural town thirty minutes south of Montreal in the heart of "SAWP country."

Although the staff at the Centre d'appui have more time in the winter to make links with other organizations supporting migrant workers, much of their resources are devoted to front-line work — giving workers basic information about their rights, helping with claim forms and advising them on employer grievances ranging from substandard housing to the denial of medical care. The risks for those who stand up for their rights or bring in the Centre d'appui are considerable. "If workers call us about a repatriation or injury, we tell them we can intervene, but evaluate the cost because, if we do, your boss will target you. So we try to support them in a way that makes our intervention less obvious," one organizer told us. Supporting workers so they can defend themselves involves basic rights education, encouraging solidarity and helping workers devise strategies for everyday acts of resistance. "We try to enforce that alone they can't change anything," she explains. "Keep together — if it's always one person that says something they'll get targeted, so approach the boss in groups of three, rotate week to week. There are small victories." The following anecdote illustrates the point:

> One employee had put Kool-aid in the water dispenser. The foreman came in yelling and insulting them and [telling them] to stop putting flavour crystals in the dispenser — that they would break it. So one of the workers spoke back, and said, "If it breaks, I'll fix it — but you can't just come into our house and talk to us like that." So the next day the foreman targeted him and said, "You! Today you don't go out working" — and the entire gang refused to work. So then the farmer came in to find out what was going on. He told them, '"You don't scare me. I'll get Agrijobs [day labourers] to replace you and send you all back to Mexico!" The workers said, "Fine!" Then that night he came back and said, "OK, what do you want?" They said, "We want an apology." So the farmer came back with pizza for everyone and publicly apologized, but that's one out of ten times. — Susanna, a Centre d'appui organizer

After five years of support and organizing work, the efforts of the Centre d'appui, and of workers such as Hector, are seeing results. "When I started last year, workers were scared to come in [to the Centre d'appui]. They would walk by and look, then not come in. Now they come and they aren't scared about their foreman seeing them come in," Susanna (an organizer) told us in 2007. She has noted some improvements in housing and that some employers have stopped confiscating workers' documents. Non-governmental organizations like Amnesty International and the Fédération des Femmes du Quebec have begun working on the issue, and there has been constant media attention. "But if the changes happen," she says, "it's at an individual level. There are no institutions or structures pushing those improvements."

In fact, it would seem the structures coordinating the SAWP/TFWP act consciously to maintain poor working conditions. The Canadian government has routinely failed to act on recommendations made by the UFCW, North-South Institute, the Canadian Labour Congress and others to improve the situation for workers; and the current expansion of the TFWP undermines the meagre protections ensured to workers via the SAWP. As noted earlier, FERME has publicly stated that it is recruiting workers from Colombia and Central America in order to undermine unionizing efforts.

> There are bosses who try to help. One said, "We are forced to adhere to the conditions imposed by the people in charge of the program. We have no power to change things. If we complain, then we get excluded from the program; so I either get my labour or not, and if I don't get them I have to sell the farm." — Centre d'appui organizer

This year's opening of the Agriculture Workers Alliance (AWA) Support Centre in St-Rémi represents a major victory. In previous years, because no one in St-Rémi would rent them office space, the Centre d'appui worked out of a trailer. Finding a place where they were allowed to park was no easy feat. Susanna told us this story to illustrate how unwelcome their efforts have been in St-Rémi:

> Finally we found a place to park where we weren't next to any houses. And these city councillors came and told us, "We've had complaints that the Mexicans 'bother' people… We don't mind that they come and work here, buy things here. It's good for the economy, but it bothers people when they hang around. So we'd like you to move so you can work in peace…" It was really hard to see them talk that way without realizing what they were saying.

For Susanna, the overt racism she witnesses in the context of her work speaks to a larger need: "There are bosses who treat workers horrendously; but it's not just that. It's the entire social context in the region that condones it. It's hard to work in those conditions, as someone who's trying to improve things — the entire social context works against it."

If the racist tone of the current social context has not been set by Canadian policy, it is certainly reinforced and condoned by it. In assigning migrant agricultural workers temporary status with no claims towards eventual permanent residency, the SAWP and TFWP define them as "not part of our community" and, in a sense, undeserving of the respect and protections afforded other workers. It is a policy that treats migrants as mere commodities, valued solely for their contributions to the Canadian economy and awarded none of the rights and privileges that come with membership in this political community.

This is not the position of the labour movement, which has by and large taken up the cause of migrant workers, seeing them as a crucial front-line in the fight to defend and improve working conditions in Canada. Of the major unions, the UFCW has been particularly active in supporting migrant agricultural workers, bringing their situation and struggles into public view, calling for reforms to the program, challenging legislation, funding support centres for workers and organizing towards unionization. In Quebec, their efforts are joined by faith-based groups, NGOs and activists who emphasize the need to facilitate workers' self-organizing and who encourage them to join wider campaigns for immigrant rights and to link with groups challenging wider neoliberal policies in Canada and in sending countries.

An ever-growing chorus is demanding fundamental reforms to the SAWP and TFWP. These include removing the hyper-restrictions associated with TFWP and SAWP work permits, which tie workers to a single employer and bar them from making immigration claims; allowing workers a voice in contract negotiations by including the UFCW as their representative; and creating an impartial process of appeal available to workers before repatriations are made. Such reforms would likely decrease the amount of workers' rights violations occurring within the programs. Growers claim such change would also bring fundamental changes to agriculture in Canada, making large-scale production untenable under the industry's current structure. Critics of the food system, who view the current agricultural model — with its reliance on agro-chemicals, export-orientation of production and concentration of corporate ownership — as a threat to food security might argue such fundamental change is long overdue.

Notes

1. The program is considered a benchmark for good practice. See Robington, Weston and de Masellis 2004.
2. Mimeault and Simard's 1999 study gives a fascinating account of the UPA's (Union des Producteurs Agricoles) Service d'emploi agricole (SEA) program, the structure, modalities and working conditions of which offer striking resemblances to the SAWP.
3. Fruit, vegetable and flower production are more labour-intensive compared to sectors such as field crops like wheat or canola, or animal production where economies of scale are possible through farmer investments in mechanization — and farmer debt.
4. Grenada, St Kitts and Nevis, Barbados, Trinidad and Tobago, Antigua, Dominica, St Lucia, St Vincent and the Grenadines, and Montserrat.

Chapter 6

Canada's Live-In Caregiver Program
Popular among Both Employers and Migrants
— But Structured for Dependency and Inequality

Throughout Canadian history, the economy has benefited from gendered and racialized labour importation to fill labour shortages (Iacovetta, Draper and Ventresca 1998). In the seventeenth century we imported *les Filles du roi*, it was Irish maids in the eighteenth and nineteenth centuries and it was Finnish ones in the early twentieth century. British women were the next wave of migrant domestic workers: their migration lasted right up until the mid-1950s. In contrast to the treatment of early migrant domestics, British women were granted full citizenship upon arrival. Canada has always benefited from the domestic labour of migrant women workers and continues to do so (Macklin 1992; Basok 2007). Today, however, the globalization of the international economy has changed the nature of the relationship between sending and receiving countries. Both Canada and source countries have implemented separate yet complementary policies and practices that regulate this international movement of labour, ensuring the regulation of migrants' labour and earnings through policies that act as de facto international "trade agreements." Wider socio-economic changes related to family structure have created both a demand in rich countries for "caregiving" workers and a supply from poor countries of female migrant workers.

In this chapter, we will discuss Canada's Live-In Caregiver Program (LCP) as an economic policy: we will examine its implications for the women who migrate to Canada under its framework. We will focus on the experience of the Filipino community: not only do they form the largest contingent of migrant caregivers, but the Philippine government has also instituted a number of policies encouraging and regulating its citizens' emigration for work opportunities. Nannies and caregivers have become part of Canada's social and economic landscape: they are now employed by a broader spectrum of Canadian families than in the past. Today, middle class families are employing migrant caregivers in order to free up Canadian women from their traditional responsibilities of child and elder care, so that they can join the paid workforce.

The rights of migrant caregivers have become an important, yet divisive, issue for Canadian feminists. There is wide insistence on Canadian women's right to work outside the home and not to be held responsible for all caregiving functions within the family. Yet, in the absence of an affordable, universal and unionized daycare system, it is difficult to achieve the goal of women having the free choice to work outside the home without leaning on low-cost migrant caregivers. Our current economy encourages us to pit one group of women's labour and human rights against another's.

As part of our project we interviewed a number of LCP workers and members of their families. Their experiences highlight the many challenges facing the women who aim to use the LCP to improve the economic and social security of their immediate and extended families. We will begin by providing an overview of the historical and political context of the LCP while delving into the experiences of women who migrate under the LCP. Their reasons for migrating, their ambiguous relationships with their employers and the outright violation of their labour rights that they sometimes experienced will be discussed. The policy barriers encountered throughout their trajectory and their life after the program will be explored. We will conclude the chapter with a reflection on the gendered nature of the LCP before turning to a case study of the work of one community group, PINAY (Filipino Women's Organization in Quebec), in its efforts to support women under the program and to advocate for its abolition.

Historical and Political Context of the LCP

As mentioned above, Canada's Live-In Caregiver Program is one of the latest in a long line of programs intended to import migrant workers, including those specifically imported for domestic work. This form of work has always tended to be a field out of which women transition as soon as they have the opportunity to do so. Domestic work is historically undervalued: it involves very difficult working conditions and few benefits. For this reason, Canadian women tend not to provide a reliable labour pool to fill the demand. Throughout our history, since Canadian women have seen live-in work as highly undesirable, those seeking live-in help have been forced to recruit outside the country.

The Caribbean Domestics Scheme, a series of bilateral agreements instituted as of 1955, facilitated the immigration of women domestic workers from the Caribbean Commonwealth countries. Under this agreement, single, childless women in good health, principally from Barbados and Jamaica, were able to come to work as nannies and maids (Barber 1991; Daenzer 1993; Stasiulis and Bakan 1997a, 1997b, 2005). Interestingly, these early domestic worker migrants were granted permanent residency upon arrival, as it was seen as discriminatory (even tantamount to forced labour) to treat them as other than regular immigrants (Blackett 2008). The immediate granting of permanent residency was removed, however, with the replacement of the Caribbean Domestics Scheme with the Foreign Domestics Movement (FDM) in 1981. This resulted in migrant women being expected to work for two years before being able to apply for permanent residency from within Canada (Stasiulis and Bakan 2005; Oxman-Martinez, Hanley and Cheung 2004).

Over the years, the identification of certain nationalities or ethnic groups as "good nannies" or "good domestic workers" has shifted, with a continuing racialization of the profession. The problems of family separation that appear when migrant domestic workers are finally reunited with their children and spouses, as well as the tendency for groups to become more assertive of their labour rights, and more organized as a community, as they become more established in Canada have been argued to be the motivating factor behind the sharp turn away from Caribbean domestic workers to Filipina ones in recent decades (Bakan and Stasiulis 1995; Basok 2007).

Not to be ignored in all of this is the role of the governments of source countries in promoting labour export as a means of relieving social pressure at home and also, as migrants send remittances home to family members, increasing foreign currency revenues. The Caribbean members of the Commonwealth had this as a clear development strategy in the 1950s (Basok 2007). Today the Philippines has surpassed all other countries as the leading source of migrant workers (Rodriguez 2002; Velasco 2002).

The Live-In Caregiver as a Labour Import Policy

Since 1992, the Live-In Caregiver Program (LCP) has served as the framework for this international flow of labour to meet the shortage of affordable child and elder live-in care (Arat-Koç 1999). The program is set up so that if individuals (overwhelmingly women) migrate to Canada and complete twenty-four months of live-in caregiver work in a government-approved employer's home within a three-year period, then these women have the right to apply from within Canada to become permanent residents. Since they have already proven their ability to work and live in Canada, most applications by live-in caregivers are automatically approved. For migrant women, this eventual acceptance as a permanent resident constitutes the main appeal of the LCP. Since the educational and capital requirements of our current immigration laws rarely permit women to enter the country as independent immigrants, the LCP is one of the only options legally open to women without capital or skills recognized as economically beneficial to Canada.

As once stated in Citizenship and Immigration Canada (CIC) documents, "The Live-In Caregiver Program exists only because there is a shortage of Canadians to fill the need for live-in care work. There is no shortage of Canadian workers available for caregiving positions where there is no live-in requirement" (CIC 1999: 2). As live-in caregivers, migrant workers may be responsible for child care, elder care, cooking, cleaning and any number of other household tasks. The requirements for eligibility are stringent, demanding post-secondary education and formal training or two years of experience in domestic and caregiving work. The process of selection is extremely stressful for applicants, whose family hopes rely upon their acceptance. One woman described how competitive the process was:

> Well, [we had to do] personal interviews and some questions on the papers. 'Cause during that time, it was hard to get in… They also did a lie test. A lot of applicants would flunk… only three passed the exams when I took them, out of fifty. That was for domestic workers; the Domestic Workers Movement [FDM] before LCP. That was in June 1984 when I came. — Bing

For the over 90 percent of LCP workers who are Filipino (CIC 2005), the governmental Philippine Overseas Employment Administration (POEA) claims to protect migrant workers' rights while bringing in $8 billion U.S. a year, much of which is used to pay off foreign debts (Roque 2005; Parreñas 2001b: 54; POEA 2001). Since 1973, in fact, with the support and encouragement of the International Monetary Fund and the World Bank, the Philippine government has been implementing what is commonly termed its Labour Export Program (Diocson 2001). In today's version of the program, the POEA facilitates training of live-in caregivers and other workers; its Government Placement Branch (GPB) helps foreign employers recruit Filipino workers (POEA 2001).

This reciprocity of labour import (Canada) and export (Philippines) policies suggests that the LCP offers an excellent opportunity to analyze Canada's use of labour import policies to participate in the globalizing economy. It would also be valuable to explore how Canada (via the LCP) may benefit from the IMF-World Bank imposed Structural Adjustment Program in the Philippines, which entails cut-backs in public health services delivery and contribute to the surplus of health care professionals (especially nurses) who migrate under the LCP (Rosen 2001).

Experience of Women Who Migrate under the LCP

Our project allowed us to interview several women who migrated under the LCP, in addition to other members of the families who were subsequently sponsored, all of whom were Filipino. There are approximately 800 Filipinos arriving annually under this program in Quebec and another approximately 500 under the family class (a category allowing workers accepted as permanent residents to sponsor their family members) not to mention other categories of workers (Ministère de l'immigration et des communautés culturelles [MICC] 2008). Within Canada as a whole, Filipinos are the third largest group of immigrants, with nearly 18,000 arriving in 2006 (CIC 2007). Our analysis of the interview data as well as our reflection on the practice experience at the Immigrant Workers Centre (IWC), brought out interesting themes related to women's reasons for using the LCP as a migration channel, their ambiguous relationships with their employers (including labour rights violations), the policy barriers they encountered and their life after the LCP was completed. In this section, we present the perspectives of the people we interviewed, using their words as much as possible.

Reasons for Migrating under the LCP

The people we interviewed told us that the LCP was one of the only feasible immigration channels available for women who wanted to come to Canada. Migration from the Philippines has long been feminized, with women going around the world — but especially to the Middle East and the industrialized countries of East Asia — in order to work as maids, nannies, nurses and other types of caregivers (Chang and Ling 2000). The Filipinas we spoke with told us that Canada is seen as nearly the best opportunity for women seeking this type of work since it is one of the only countries that offers permanent residency and the eventual possibility of being accompanied by family members at the end of the road (Chang and Ling 2000).

Applying for permanent residency as an independent immigrant did not seem like a good option to the people to whom we spoke. Although most of those we spoke to did fit the basic points criteria of Citizenship and Immigration Canada, they didn't believe that their qualifications would be fairly evaluated: also, most importantly, the LCP gave them the opportunity to start earning much more quickly than the usual immigration channels. Under the LCP, it is possible to get to Canada within six months, at which point they can immediately start earning and sending money home. An immigration application takes a minimum of two years: it can sometimes take even longer when the application is going through Manila.

The relative speed of the LCP is a major draw to the potential migrants to Canada given the lack of economic opportunity in the Philippines or other source countries. For women to be able to make Canadian dollars and send them back to the family to pay for basic things like quality health care and education is an opportunity that has an impact beyond the migrant herself. As a result, women often face heavy pressure from their families to make sacrifices that benefit them all. Rudy tells us how this shaped her decision to come:

> I came to Canada from the Philippines when I was twenty-two. I only had two semesters left of my university psychology degree, but my mother was really encouraging me. She was already in Canada working as an LCP and she found me a job with her employer's friend. She said I shouldn't give up the opportunity to come to Canada, so I immigrated as part of the Live-In Caregiver Program. — Rudy

LCP migrants had high hopes for the future of their families. Women were highly motivated to be able to have their children complete their education in Canada: they hoped this would help them achieve future success. They imagined that their children would quickly integrate into Canadian society and end up pursuing higher education and professional jobs as they had done back in the Philippines. In Canada, however, they expected these kinds of jobs to bring their kids good enough incomes so that they would not have to migrate again. In some cases, and especially among the youngest women who did not have any direct dependents at home, a desire for new experiences was their main reason for coming to Canada to work.

Ambiguous Relationships with Employer

Once in Canada, LCP workers reported having very ambiguous relationships with their employers. Some of them felt lucky to have had good employers: they told us that they had a sense of being part of the family and that their employers encouraged them to take the steps necessary to have a secure life in Canada by, for example, pursuing their education. Many women we spoke to felt grateful to their employer for having sponsored them to come to Canada, a feeling they said their employers encouraged. The flip side of such feelings, however, was a sense of discomfort in talking about employment issues such as pay, work hours and vacation time.

When it came to the people they cared for, whether children or adults, the women said they often developed sincere feelings for them, even love. These feelings were juxtaposed against a resentment about being separated from their own children or loved ones in order to care for someone else's family. While the relationship with the care recipient was usually fairly good, LCP workers often felt a lack of respect from the employer, typically the children's parents or the children of a dependent senior. Several women reported that they really felt taken for granted, or worse:

> I am not happy working with these people who have no satisfaction with me. I don't like this. They treated me like an idiot because I came from another country, because you are not Canadian like them. — Ilga

Isolation is another issue for LCP workers. Although technically, they are not required to remain in the employer's home beyond their official work hours, most women were expected to be on call in the home twenty-four hours a day, with the exception of their day and a half off over the weekend. Expected to be in the home, yet not fully integrated into family activities, many LCP workers felt very lonely. Given their limited time off, they also had a difficult time making and maintaining relationships with family and friends in the broader community in Montreal.

What was most upsetting to one of the women we interviewed was that the loneliness, isolation and control were invisible to her employer. She felt they didn't think about how she might be feeling and considered it normal for her to work all the time "since she's at home anyway." At the same time, she didn't feel she could do anything:

> A lot of Filipinos and others are silent in their jobs... they don't say anything in their jobs even if they are exploited because they are scared... they are scared that if they do something for change, they will be deported... especially those who are in the Live-In Caregiver Program, and even those with immigrant status, they are scared to be terminated. They feel held at the blade between life and death. — Ilga

In some cases, the exploitation of LCP workers' labour and human rights is very clear. They often work long hours with no overtime pay, are not free to leave home during their "off" hours, and their movements and communications are controlled by the employer. Rudy's first job is an example of this kind of employer:

> My first employer was really demanding. They expected me to push the boundaries of my job description, going on vacations with the family, overtime without pay, taking care of the family dog when they went out of town. At first I was submissive and went along with what they asked. I was kind of submissive — it's in our culture. But I got tired of it and I started to stand up for myself on the job as I learned about my rights. — Rudy

When LCP workers don't follow the unwritten rules, then things become very difficult for them, sometimes making it nearly impossible for them to work — a situation with serious consequences for the migrant's immediate welfare, their future immigration possibilities and the well-being of their family back at home. Getting pregnant before the LCP is finished causes major difficulties for women migrants:

> When I came to Canada, I didn't know I was pregnant because I passed the medical exam [for Citizenship and Immigration Canada]. Even when I found out I was pregnant, I kept on looking for a job. But I could not hide it from employers because my tummy got big! I told them I was capable of doing it. But they still rejected me because of that. And when I had the baby, it was still a problem. — Ilga

Policy Barriers Encountered

LCP migrants face a number of very specific barriers when it comes to exercising their rights under Canadian social programs. Labour rights — whether it be labour standards, health and safety or employment insurance — are tenuous for LCP workers. In terms of labour standards, for example, LCP workers find themselves in a difficult position should they wish to make a claim. If the provincial code includes domestic workers under the regular labour standards legislation (in Quebec they have only been fully covered since 2003), then LCP workers should have exactly the same rights as any other worker. In practice, however, their specific work conditions make it difficult for them to exercise these rights. Ilga explains:

> Yes, but the Labour Standards said that I needed a witness [to prove] that when the employer was away if I was really working for the whole day during this period in the house. I needed a witness to have grounds to win a case regarding this employer. I offered them my diary which recorded my working hours but I still needed a witness. I thought, where am I going to get a witness? I can't afford to hire a witness to watch me while I'm working just so that they can prove it! [she is laughing.] So I didn't have a case to get the employer to pay me overtime, because I didn't have a witness. How can you have a witness in a private home with a small amount of salary?! — Ilga

Another example of how women's work is not properly included in the usual labour protections is that, in the province of Quebec, domestic work is explicitly excluded from compensation in the case of a work-related accident or illness. Therefore, all LCP workers in Quebec are currently left to deal with medical expenses, loss of income and possibly loss of capacity to work, if they get hurt on the job.

The other barrier to exercising full labour rights is the carrot at the end of the LCP stick — permanent residency. Rita said:

> For a long time, I knew the rules and wanted to go complain to the Normes de Travail [Labour Standards Commission] but I was afraid to lose my job. I

worked like a buffalo because I wanted permanent residency and I didn't want to risk losing that job. — Rita

Immigration status causes major problems for LCP workers. Should a worker have to change employer — for example, should an elderly employer die, should the employer run out of money, or should the worker and employer have conflicts between them — an LCP worker must look for a new employer and apply for a new employer-specific visa. The delay can easily be upwards of six months, during which time, the worker finds herself in a "grey zone" of immigration status. As long as her thirty-six months are not up, she will not be deported, but, until she finds a new employer, she is cut off from many benefits. Medicare benefits may be cut off if the migrant is unemployed, for example, and, in Quebec, the worker may be subjected to a three-month waiting period once she reapplies for Medicare with a new employer's visa. For Ilga, one of the rare LCP workers to have a dependent in Canada (her son was born here shortly after her arrival), this problem extended beyond herself:

> Because every time I lost my paper, my son lost his Medicare card too. My son had to follow my status. — Ilga

This "grey zone" of immigration also causes problems for LCP workers who seek Employment Insurance when they lose their jobs. EI staff often refuse them benefits, using the argument that, unless they have a valid work permit, they cannot legally work in Canada. However, LCP workers cannot receive a valid work permit until they have already found an employer!

Life after the LCP

Unfortunately, LCP migrants' hopes for a better future rarely pan out in the short to medium term. Many LCP workers remain in domestic work in the short term once their program is finished because their immigration procedures are expensive and the domestic work is a relatively sure thing. Those who do exit domestic work mostly seem to end up working in factories or doing low-paid service work. For those who had difficulties with their employers, the search for a better job can be very difficult:

> Yes, but every time I had an interview, they wanted references from my old employer. And they were bad references, either because I didn't get along with my employer or because no one thinks domestic work is real work! — Rita

For Filipinos, it is rare to have educational qualifications and experience from back home recognized as valid in Canada. This was a real disappointment to one man who was sponsored on the LCP by his wife:

> Not only Filipinos, but a lot of immigrants, a lot of children and youth are in the streets [hanging out] because of this. They finished their studies down there but when they come here, they have to go back to school because its not recognized... So what are they supposed to do? They will be in the streets

and they will work low-paid jobs. — Amado

Although permanent residency does not provide the magic answer for LCP workers, not obtaining it can mean deportation, restarting the program, migrating to another country or going underground, none of which are very palatable options to people doing their best to support families back home and create a better future for their children:

> When I got kicked out of my employer's place, I asked if I could call a taxi. But the employer said that he didn't know the number of the taxi, and he was smiling behind my back, I saw. But I just called that nanny and asked her to call me a taxi, so she is the one who called the taxi. The taxi took me to another friend that I knew from Egypt [where she had worked before coming to Canada]. The recruitment agency knew that friend, and called me there, leaving a message that because I didn't finish my three months, she was going to call immigration and try to deport me, and that I wouldn't find another job. She threatened me! — Ilga

Obtaining permanent residency is long and expensive, and many LCP workers do not manage to meet the basic requirements:

> [Citizenship and Immigration Canada] was asking me to leave voluntarily because I wasn't able to fulfill the requirements of the Live-In Caregiver Program. In three years, I only had eleven months out of twenty-four. Because after three years, you need to apply for a permanent residence… with a processing fee of $500. If you don't apply they will say you are not interested in staying in Canada. — Ilga

The deskilling of the LCP and the related difficulties of obtaining permanent residency has even been suggested as a push towards marriage with Canadians (McKay 2003).

For those who do manage to stay and sponsor their families, relationships with spouses and children are often difficult upon reunification (Cohen 2000; Parreñas 2001a). A lot of families subsequently break up. The delay between a woman leaving the Philippines and the eventual reunification of the family can easily be six years. Nadine, a teenager who was sponsored by her mother, talks about how she copes with this tension:

> It helps that I learned to see my family's situation in a political — and not just a personal — context. Now I'm not as hurt or angry that my mother has to work fourteen-hour days and can't spend much time with me. Now I see my mother's long working hours as a part of the Canadian economy that takes advantage of cheap immigrant labour. Reunification with our mother has been even harder for my younger brother. I feel bad for my brother — he was just a baby [when her mother left], he never knew my mother. Most of my friends in the Filipino community share the same situation. In high school, one of my friends would run away from home almost every month. — Nadine

Not surprisingly, the number of women running into difficulty under the LCP has led to the rise of collective action for their rights. In Montreal, PINAY is a well-known grassroots organization working for the rights of Filipina women. In the next section, we offer a case study of PINAY based on interviews with several of its members and an analysis of its documents.

Organizing around the LCP: A Case Study of PINAY

Pinay is a Filipino word to describe a Filipina woman living outside of the Philippines. Usually, when Filipinos meet Filipina women outside their country they ask, "*Pinay ka ba* (Are you Pinay)?" PINAY, the association, is a non-profit organization of Filipina migrant and immigrant women workers created in 1991 in response to the need to organize and empower Filipina women in Quebec. Since then, it has played a role in the fight for the rights and welfare of Filipino migrants and immigrants, especially Filipina domestic workers and their families living and working in Quebec.

Since its inception, PINAY has united many female domestic workers and their allies in the hard struggle for the protection of all Canadian Filipino immigrant workers' well-being and of their rights. It has also successfully developed a vast network of allies among diverse women's organizations, at both a national and an international level.

Filipina LCP workers have unique concerns and conditions, such as:

- economic segregation of Filipina women and disproportionate poverty among the entire population including second-generation youth;
- long periods of family separation;
- de-skilling and stalled development (for example, professionally trained Filipinas working as domestics, factory workers and other jobs unrelated to their training);
- systemic racism and discrimination, including denial of basic benefits, services and resources; and
- all forms of violence and abuse.

"Sacrificing Is the Way to Get to Heaven"

The creation of PINAY was a result of a study done by a master's level student in the McGill School of Social Work. Thelma de Jesus decided to conduct research on the working conditions of Filipina domestic workers and caregivers. The focus group discussions during the work on the thesis raised awareness of the need for the participants to create a support group. "Only then," said one of the participants, "when answering to these questions, we realized that we were facing so many problems. We understood that we need each other in order to promote our work conditions."

The meetings of the group were held in different places each time, usually in private homes or coffee shops. The objective of that support group was to share their experiences as domestic and caregiver workers and to empower themselves while gathering information. "Back then, it was more a social gathering than a political one," says one of the participants. After a while, the participants realized that, since they shared so many challenges that are common to Filipina domestic workers and caregivers, there was a need to establish an organization that would not only empower the workers but would also advocate and promote their rights.

At that time, what is known today as the LCP was called the Foreign Domestics Movement. The regulations were different than today. In the first version of the program, live-in domestics and caregivers were not included in Quebec Labour Standards. For example, they had to work a higher fixed number of working hours per week than other Quebeckers before becoming eligible for overtime pay; as well there were no maximum hours in a workweek, there was no minimum wage, and the workers did not have any work contract. Furthermore, in cases of human rights violations or in cases of abuse (sexual, verbal or physical) by their employer, there was no mechanism in place for them to complain about it to any formal authorities, nor any means to get compensation. One PINAY member said:

> Back then, it was very difficult for us to even think about changing the situation, because it meant to stand up for your rights, to fight with your employers and with the government. A lot of us were not prepared to do it.

It is not simple to fight for your rights, says another member,

> because you are afraid that if you complain, then you will be deported. But apart from that, it's that the Filipinos have a cultural challenge to resist, to rebel. Especially the Filipino women, most of us believe that sacrificing is the way to get to heaven. It is according to our religious and cultural beliefs: Don't complain, don't be critical. In the Philippines, you do what you are told. You can't rebel against your parents; they are deciding for you what to do and what you would learn, because they are the ones who are paying for the school. After you finish with your studies, you feel guilty because they have spent so much money on you, so then you have to pay them back by working abroad and sending them the money. So there's no way you can rebel at your work, even if they shout at you, or humiliate you. You automatically feel guilty. It takes a lot of time to change this attitude and to develop awareness.

The Triumph of Melca Salvador

In 1996, PINAY was officially founded as a non-profit organization: Tess Agustin was appointed as its chair. Members of PINAY say that the first issue that bothered the members in PINAY's earlier days was the time needed to get permanent resident status. Considering the many negative elements of the previous program, the main benefit under the Foreign Domestic Movement was that they would get their status after six months of work. This policy was changed in 1992, when the Mulroney government implemented the LCP: the new program required twenty-four months of live-in work before being able to apply to immigrate.

Since then, PINAY has been responsible for or participated in many other campaigns. Some of them were through alliance work. For example, PINAY participated in the Bread and Roses March in 1995 held by the Women's Federation of Quebec (Fédération des femmes du Quebec — FFQ). PINAY collaborates with the South Asian Women's Community Centre (SAWCC); in 1998 PINAY participated in the National Action Committee on the Status of Women. In 2000, PINAY participated in Quebec City for the World March of Women. In 2002, and ever since, PINAY has played a leadership role in the celebrations of International Women's Day with the March 8th Committee of Women of Diverse Origins. PINAY also cooperates with the AAFQ (Association des aides familiales du Quebec). It participated in consultation meetings with international bodies such as the U.N. Rapporteur on the Rights of Migrant Workers and their Families in 2002 and on Racism, Discrimination and Xenophobia in 2003. PINAY is also a member organization of the National Alliance of Philippine Women in Canada, which lobbies the federal government for the protection of migrant workers and their families.

However, through the years, PINAY was also initiating its own campaigns. In 1999, PINAY launched the Quebec Purple Rose Campaign to "Stop Sex Trafficking of Filipino Women and Children." Yet the most famous campaign done by PINAY was in 2001, the "Stop the Expulsion of Melca Salvador Campaign." At that time, Salvador, a former LCP worker, was the vice chair of PINAY. While under the LCP, Salvador told her employer that she was pregnant: she was promptly fired. As a result, she was only able to complete eleven months of live-in work out of the required twenty-four. Therefore, in 2001, she was about to be deported.

As one of the campaign participants describes it:

> For four months every Tuesday we were demonstrating in front of the Canadian immigration building, until the decision to deport her was cancelled. We also had some help from other organizations across Canada such as the National Action Committee for the Status of Women. It was the first time that our issue became a public interest. The Melca Salvador Campaign strengthened us a lot. The general public and also more Filipinos got to know us.

The success of the campaign was two-fold. Not only did the campaign keep Melca and her son in Canada, but it also helped expose the oppression and exploitation of the LCP workers.

Another Achievement: LCP Workers Are
Included in the Regular Quebec Labour Standards

Since the "Melca Salvador Campaign," PINAY had another remarkable accomplishment. In 2003, PINAY worked with the FDNS (Front de défense des non-syndiqués) to win a campaign to include domestic workers under Quebec Labour Standards (Normes de travail) and to amend the Labour Standards to improve the rights and protection of all workers, particularly migrant workers.

For the LCP workers, this meant they were eligible, for the first time, for the same minimum wage as other workers and to receive overtime pay after a forty-hour week. As a result, LCP workers were able now to file claims to get paid for overtime work: they also gained the option to file a complaint if their rights were violated, and to be compensated.

Other campaigns that PINAY is involved with are linked to the change of immigration policies, labour policies and political issues. PINAY lobbies Citizenship and Immigration Canada and federal politicians to scrap what PINAY sees as a racist and anti-women immigration policy in the LCP. Instead, they advocate a more equitable and quicker process that would allow Filipinos to come in as landed immigrants. PINAY also responded publicly against the unscrupulous recruitment agency (the name says it all: "Diva International") which advertised an online auctioning of Filipina domestic workers in the *Montreal Gazette* in 2003. At the same time they were lobbying both the provincial and federal governments to take action on this issue.

In 2005, PINAY participated in the Citizenship and Immigration Canada roundtable discussion on the LCP. In 2006, PINAY presented a paper on the trafficking of women in the context of forced labour. This paper was based on PINAY's experiences and it made recommendations to a panel of government representatives from an Inter-Ministerial Committee formed by the Minister of Justice, and later to a panel of government representatives created by the Quebec Minister of Immigration and Cultural Communities.

Sometimes PINAY's campaigns are also directed towards decision makers in the Philippines. For example, in 2006, PINAY protested against President Gloria Macapagal Arroyo, who, according to PINAY, has plundered the Philippine economy and has driven Filipinos to migrate because of poverty and the lack of jobs in the Philippines. It is interesting to note that members of PINAY have differing opinions on how the Filipino community perceives its activities. Some indicate that PINAY is seen by the community as a troublemaker and as an organization that gives a bad image to the Filipino community in the eyes of the Canadian public and decision makers: "We are too much of activists in their opinion. They think we should be quiet and submissive." Other PINAY members say that this was true a few years ago, but that recently the Filipino community's attitude towards PINAY has become more supportive and positive.

We Ask Ourselves: "How Come We Ended Up Here as Domestic Workers?"

Either way, with or without the support of the mainstream Filipino community, PINAY has grown over the years from a small support group into a structured organization. The structure has changed throughout the years, from a group that sometimes had a chairperson to its current version: PINAY's executive is composed of a chairperson (in 2008, Evelyn Calugay), a vice chair (Delia de Veyra) and two committee heads: the organizing and finance committee (chaired by Tess Agustin) and the education committee (chaired by Jasmin de la Calzada). Each committee head is responsible for recruiting as many as members as she likes to her committee. Once a month there is an executive meeting, in addition to monthly committee meetings.

The main role of the education committee is to facilitate different kinds of workshops. According to Evelyn, "We try to reach out to more domestic workers through our workshops, especially about the labour regulations, so they will be able to demand their rights and to recognize any violations." Apart from the educational discussions on Quebec work standards for home caregivers, the other workshops are on the subjects of immigration policies, income taxes, organizing and mobilization, the history of the Philippines (which includes discussion on the political situation that causes so many Filipinos to leave), writing newsletters, media awareness and popular theatre.

> In the workshops, we ask the women to open up their minds, to learn, not to be isolated. It took me fifty years to realize that I was exploited. I don't want these young women to wait fifty years to understand this. I don't want them to go through what I have been going through. During our meetings we ask ourselves: "How come we ended up here as domestic workers?" It is not easy to change the way people were brought up, and not all of them have the will to change their submissive perspective.

Since PINAY is a non-profit organization, the members decided that there was a need for a finance and organizing committee. The main goal of the committee has been to raise more money by planning fund-raising activities such as apple picking in the summer, selling raffle tickets and the annual Christmas party. Another important activity of the committee is to add more members to PINAY.

The Challenge: Recruiting New Members

In order to be helped by PINAY one doesn't have to be a member, nor a Filipino. Nevertheless, since 1991, PINAY has signed up over 500 members. Because of the nature of the life of LCP workers, membership is a difficult thing to sustain. Some people go back to the Philippines soon after they arrive in Canada; others get their permanent status and leave for a different region in Canada, mainly because they lack the fluency in French that is needed in Quebec; and other members come to PINAY only when they face a problem personally. "When that is being solved, they disappear," one of the members says bitterly. There are usually between twenty and thirty active members who are politically involved. The rest, about a hundred people, participate in activities occasionally. Active members pay a membership fee of $10.

New members are recruited through word of mouth, through participation and outreach in events within the Filipino community (usually in the summertime), through the different workshops given by the education committee and through referrals done by other organizations. PINAY's newsletter is also a means of reaching out to more Filipino domestic workers. PINAY sends it by email and distributes it as a hard copy, especially during community events. In the newsletter, there are articles about different PINAY activities and its services.

Influencing Public Opinion

One of the earliest ways that PINAY tried to reach out to more domestic workers, but also to the general public, was by writing, coordinating and presenting a popular theatre play on the history of Filipino migrant worker struggles. All of the participants were Filipino migrant workers and their children. The play was performed in 1995 at the Maison de la Culture in Montreal's Côte-des-Neiges neighbourhood, the heart of the Filipino community. PINAY tried to demonstrate, through theatre, the way that Filipina women lost their power and became submissive after the Spanish invasion, as well as their situation today in the LCP. In 1997, they mounted a second play, "Kababaihang Pilipina Noon, Ngayon at Bukas" (Filipino Women Yesterday, Today and Tomorrow).

Throughout the years, PINAY has used the media as a powerful tool to reach out mainly to the general public and to decision makers. In 1993, PINAY participated and assisted in the launching of two films by Productions Multi-Monde entitled "Brown Women, Blonde Babies" and "When Strangers Reunite." In 1994, they produced a radio documentary "Exporting Lives: Stories of Filipino Migrant Workers in Canada and the Philippines," a forty-five-minute radio show that was broadcast on CKUT, McGill University's community radio station. PINAY also participated in another weekly radio show, "Cry of the People," at the same radio station: this show discussed issues and questions affecting Filipinos here and elsewhere.

In the written media, as well as in the electronic media, articles and items on PINAY appeared in *The Gazette*, CBC News, the Canada Newswire and local newspapers like *The Mirror*. Through these articles, PINAY has been able to expand public awareness, not only about PINAY itself, but also about its activities on various subjects such as fights against individual deportations, LCP work conditions, different cases of human rights violations and the lack of health and injury coverage.

Another lobbying frontier for PINAY has come about through its collaboration with the academic world. PINAY has had a very special connection to academia since its early days. Over the years it has participated in several academic research projects, such as the National Participatory Research Project on the situation of Filipino domestic workers in 1995, a community-based survey on the condition of Filipino domestic workers in Montreal and its suburbs in 1999, and a follow-up community-based survey in 2007–2008. PINAY members are currently conducting interviews about the health and work conditions of domestic workers: they are expected to reach over 160 women.

Dreaming of a Transition Home

It is a bit hard to imagine that PINAY has done all its activities throughout its sixteen years of existence without having a physical space or any staff. After all these years, PINAY still doesn't operate from an office because it cannot afford to have one. The phone of PINAY is the personal home phone of the chairperson, the meetings are held either in the office of the Immigrant Workers' Centre in

Côte-des-Neiges, in private homes or in coffee shops.

In 2000 PINAY had a "transition home" for workers under the LCP who had to run away from abusive employers. It was a place in which these women could not only seek temporary refuge, but could also meet other women in similar situations, collect data, receive counselling, have access to a legal clinic and be offered the necessary referrals. It was funded by the Anglican Church for three years. This apartment was also used as the official office of the organization. "People could come there and feel that they were belonging to something. This way we were more accessible to people," a PINAY member commented.

Unfortunately, PINAY was unable to sustain this transition home, primarily because of a lack of available or accessible resources. So, in the meantime, they have to settle for hosting women who left their employers and need immediate accommodation in the home of a PINAY member. They dream of the re-establishment of a transition home that will also function as a centre where migrant women can meet to hold workshops and educational discussions, while continuing to provide shelter to domestic workers in need.

Looking to the Future

Currently PINAY continues to be active and to participate in very interesting campaigns. In collaboration with the IWC and the AAFQ, PINAY is trying to pressure the Quebec Government to extend coverage of workers' compensation to domestic workers. Domestic workers are not covered under the law that provides employees with compensation in cases of work accidents or illnesses. PINAY representatives managed to meet with the Quebec Minister of Labour and raised with him the issue of domestic workers' right to equality under the CSST (Quebec's workers' compensation program).

Through a campaign that includes Project Genesis and the Immigrant Workers' Centre as part of its core organizing group, PINAY is also demanding the abolition of the three-month delay for Medicare coverage for newly arrived migrants/immigrants. In collaboration with these groups, PINAY demands health care for all, at all times. Currently, Medicare covers LCP workers as long as they have an employer. If they choose to leave their employer, then, until they find another employer, they are not covered.

PINAY also tries to promote more flexibility in employment for migrant workers, including demanding the cancellation of the obligation to indicate the name of the specific employer in the work permit. This campaign also includes a demand for accreditation of Filipino nurses and other professionals. Finally, PINAY tries to advocate for workers to have an option to live out. In their opinion, the live-in arrangement invites exploitation of the workers and opportunities for abuse.

Since PINAY was founded its objectives and goals have been modified. What started as a support group, providing social and emotional support to a few members, has become a political organization with a clear agenda. PINAY believes that the conditions that push millions of Filipinos seeking work abroad are linked to the injustices we face in Canada. The current objectives of PINAY centre on three areas: (1) issues related to the LCP; (2) social support; and (3) solidarity. The primary current objectives as stated by the organization are:

- to advocate and promote the rights and welfare of Filipino migrant workers;
- to participate in and support the women's movement in the Philippines working for social change and peace, based on justice; and
- to remove the conditions and barriers that stall the development of Filipino women in Quebec and Canada, and to struggle for progressive policies that benefit all people.

PINAY plans to continue its activities of holding workshops and its clinical information clinic, as well as to continue with its current campaigns. There are also more concrete objectives of PINAY for the near future:

- to develop a more structured volunteer program, in which volunteers will be committed to assist PINAY's advocacy, and services;
- to provide an annual CPR training;
- to provide a support program for women and their families in the community, to assist their integration in the new society in which they live; and
- to achieve a sustainable economic development such as home care or retail cooperatives for the women so that they are able to develop sources of income that are more independent and that allow them to use their skills and pursue their interests.

Since PINAY was founded it seems that the target audience of PINAY has been expanded. PINAY today addresses its services not only to Filipino LCP workers but also to domestic workers from other countries, as well as to women who are being trafficked. One member sums it up as follows, "Today I feel that we are fighting not only for the Filipino women, but also for all the women that are abused. We are fighting against the injustice in society towards the working class. Not only the caregivers are being exploited."

Gendered Impacts of the LCP

Research in Canada has long been documenting the gendered impacts of the LCP (Hodge 2006). Diocson (2001) points out that Filipino emigration is characterized by its feminization. Given that caregiving is traditionally women's work (Parreñas 2001b), it is not surprising that 79 percent of LCP immigrants are women (CIC 2000). It is also significant that most LCP workers are women of colour from developing countries: the top four countries of origin for LCP workers are the Philippines, Great Britain, Jamaica and Guyana (CIC 2005).

The implications of the LCP for health (Spitzer et al. 2001), professional accreditation (Osborne 2001; PWC 2001; Rosen 2001) and human trafficking (PWC 2000; Oxman-Martinez, Martinez and Hanley 2001) have been explored by researchers: initial results suggest that women who come to Canada through the LCP face many barriers to full equality. Nearly two decades ago, authors like Calliste (1991), Bolaria (1990) and Ng (1992) were already noting that these unequal power relations are a by-product of lack of union protection, inadequate labour legislation, uncertain health and safety protection and ineffective protection from physical and sexual harassment.

Of fundamental importance in understanding the pitfalls of the LCP is the program's linking of migrant women's immigration status to a male sponsor or employer. This dependency places them at particular risk for exploitation (Langevin and Belleau 2000; Côté et al. 2001). Whether or not this risk becomes reality does not lessen the importance of the limits placed on these women's human rights. LCP workers are denied the basic freedoms of choosing their place of residence and conditions of employment (Boti and Bautista 1999). It is difficult to conceive of such conditions being imposed on a majority male workforce.

According to Juteau (1997), gender relations emphasize the relationship between unpaid and paid labour, not in a unilinear continuum but as an aspect of the appropriation of women's labour whether they be native- or foreign-born. Female immigrant work is perceived as "legalized slavery" and as being part of the sex trade. This highlights the intersection between gender, race, ethnicity and class (Krane, Oxman-Martinez and Ducey 2001).

Regarding impacts on health, LCP workers have limited access to sick leave and do not qualify for state-funded Medicare as do most temporary workers. In addition, they often fall through the cracks of eligibility for welfare and/ or employment insurance if they are no longer able to work. According to La Fondation pour l'aide aux travailleurs accidentés du Quebec, access to workers' compensation is also hindered by numerous obstacles for migrant workers such as language and immigration status. In general, LCP workers enjoy a lower standard of work conditions during their initial qualification period.

Despite the research already completed, however, significant gaps remain in our understanding of the impact of this "labour import policy" on the women migrating under the LCP. While LCP workers benefit from the potential opportunity to apply for landed immigrant status from within Canada, they must first meet all of the difficult and restrictive conditions within the first three years in Canada. Such conditions may have an effect on LCP workers' future employment and integration potential. Investigation is needed to document how women LCP workers' precarious status of immigration and work conditions affect, directly or indirectly, access to better employment, financial security or economic autonomy, once they become landed immigrants in Canada. Unfortunately, it is a significant challenge to document any direct relationship between employment trajectories and the policies and practices of the LCP, since many variables influence individuals' outcomes. One study has recently been addressing this question and results should be available soon (Spitzer, Hughes, Oxman-Martinez and Hanley forthcoming).

The importance of re-examining labour import policies has increased in the wake of the September 11th attacks on the World Trade Centre and the Pentagon and the open realignment of migration policies around economic and security concerns. Many countries are revising their migration policies and Canada's LCP (with its possibility of applying for permanent residency from within the country) is being explored by other industrial countries as a possible model for the import of foreign labour (Blackell 2001). Before Canada encourages the replication of the LCP, however, it would be useful to have a better understanding of the long-term labour impacts of this policy for both the migrants involved and the host country. The literature review suggests, and our interviews fully support, that full and equal integration does not exist and that the LCP may have to be adjusted if there is a genuine political will to achieve this ideal of equality within the context of a competitive international economy.

Conclusion

Community-based research shows that one of the most onerous requirements of the Live-In Caregiver Program is actually implied in the program's name: the obligation to "live-in" at the employer's residence. As has been discussed above, this requirement creates conditions more conducive to exploitation of both labour and personal rights. Although actual occurrences may be rare, the social isolation that results from living-in nevertheless makes women more vulnerable to physical, psychological and/or sexual abuse, which harms their overall health. More common is the abuse of workers' labour rights: living in makes it next to impossible to refuse to work unpaid overtime and to insist upon basic working conditions.

The LCP's creation of a situation of dependence is another major problem. Since LCP workers' immigration status is tied to a specific employer and requires the twenty-four months of live-in service within three years, leaving an exploitative job and looking for a new position poses the risk of losing the right to remain in Canada. Consequently, many women feel the necessity to remain in abusive work situations. In recent years, there has been a rising tide of political action calling for the abolition or at least the reform of the Live-In Caregiver Program. It seems clear that removing the live-in requirement and providing for independent immigration status for migrant caregivers could lessen opportunities for the violation of their rights. Less clear are the long-term implications of the LCP for the future political and economic equality of these women within Canadian society.

Given this uncertainty about the long-term effects of the LCP, the recent trend towards more "guest-worker" programs in Canada is disturbing. The LCP, despite its many documented problems, has been extremely effective at, if nothing else, ensuring a steady supply of low-cost, compliant workers for jobs that Canadians are unwilling to take. The low pay, difficult conditions and low respect attached to caregiving and domestic work meant that Canadians give this type of employment a wide berth. The program seems so effective, in fact, that the government seems to have concluded that it would be a good idea to extend

Contesting at Work

Deena, like many others, came from the Philippines to find a better life in Canada. She had worked in Manila in a relatively good job and was thirty-one when she arrived. In the Philippines, she completed high school education and started a computer-secretarial course that she didn't finish because she began getting too busy with her immigration application. She had also developed her own business, making clocks, with the help of a former employer, which she ran for about eight years. Despite having worked in these areas, the only option for her to come to Canada was as a domestic worker under the Live-In Caregiver Program. In the Philippines, she learned what the salary was for live-ins in Canada and when she counted it in pesos, she was amazed by how much money it was. She was not told that living expenses in Canada were also quite high. She did not know anyone here except the wife of a Canadian official who had worked in the Philippines.

Canada did not live up to her expectations. Although she worked as a live-in, she was expected to rent her own place and go there on weekends. She felt alone and so on Sundays she went to church where she met other women. During the weekend, she said, "You FEEL, you mingle with all the Filipinos and get support."

In her first job, she worked for a woman for nine months. She says it was light work. She washed hair and cleaned a condo that was not too big. But the woman's son interfered with her work. He treated her "like a dog, as if I had a sickness." So, although she had a great relationship with the mother, she explained to her that she couldn't stay because of the son, and she left.

After that, she went to work for a family in Westmount (an upper-middle-class community in Montreal) who had a bigger house: three floors, seven bathrooms and three children aged nine, ten and thirteen. She stayed there for three years. In the beginning it was okay. Once she completed her two years required by the Live-In Caregiver Program, she asked her employer if she could live out and he said okay.

Under the old *Labour Standards Act*, when a live-in makes the transition to live out, the employer is supposed to pay a regular salary to reflect that the employee has additional expenses, but in Deena's case, the Westmount family refused to give her the additional money. She knew that she was supposed to be getting more money as a live-out caregiver. She said it was a rule that she learned in the Philippines when she was taught about the rules and procedures of the program.

She met her current husband, an older Quebecois man, at a party of a Filipino association. She had a daughter in the Philippines who she was eventually able to bring over to Canada. She is now twelve and living with her and her husband. With the support of her husband, she began to lose her fear because he helped her not to be afraid and encouraged her to take her case to Normes du travail. She did so seven months after she became "live-out": when she did that, her communication with the family went down. At the beginning they were very nice to her and left her food, but when she challenged their lack of payment, they stopped leaving her food. Ultimately she won the case.

After she left the Westmount family, she collected Employment Insurance until she went to work at a company that distributes medicines. She heard about the job through friends.

the general Temporary Foreign Worker Program to include workers in other industries that have a hard time recruiting reliable low-paid workers (hotel and hospital cleaners or kitchen workers, for example) or for technical jobs for which they have had to pay a premium due to the difficult conditions (meat packing, construction, remote resource extraction). The Low-Skill Pilot Project (LSPP) was hence born, incorporating many of the restrictive measures first applied under the LCP. Critics argue that the LSPP represents an accommodation of employer demand for quick recruitment and compliant workers as well as a refusal to face up to the problems in LCP.

Chapter 7

Survival and Fighting Back

In this chapter, we will explore the tensions between adapting and resisting in immigrant workers' places of work. As discussed in earlier chapters, there are huge pressures to adapt to unjust situations. Yet people resist and challenge either their employers directly or state policies that shape this exploitation. Often, resisting involves risks for the workers, as we pointed out with SAWP and LCP workers. In this chapter, we will explore the concepts of adaptation and resistance and the way people live both at the same time. Drawing from the experiences of workers whom we interviewed we look at how resignation occurs in some cases, and how people reach limits and fight back in others. We conclude with the lessons and a discussion of the politics of resistance and organizing immigrant workers.

Adaptation cannot be separated from resistance. The category of immigrant worker, as Parreñas (2001) describes in her study of Filipina domestic workers, implies both attempts to resist (attempt to eliminate) or negotiate (attempt to mitigate) the effects of dislocations in their everyday lives. Adaptation is the usual response to the situation faced by new arrivals in a country, even if they face highly exploitative working conditions with little evidence that these will change. A key element in resistance is learning; indeed, to resist is to learn. Maitra and Shan (2007) contrast two types of learning that parallel adaptation and resistance. First, conformative learning is learning that is conditioned by the expectations and requirements of the workplace as defined by employers. This type of learning is about "getting by," "holding on to a job": it generally fits in with the needs of employers to maximize profits. The second type, transgressive learning, is learning to exercise rights, to challenge and overcome exploitative work situations and enlarge opportunities for a better life. But what are the factors that lead to conformative learning? What are the connections between the larger and the immediate contexts in shaping situations and choices? As we have pointed out, there is enormous pressure for people to adapt to very difficult circumstances because they have few choices and options. We have provided many examples of this tension in immigrants' everyday lives in Canada. In this context, described earlier in the book, we will see how learning to become an immigrant worker can mean learning to live in jobs with little or no mobility, at the bottom of the labour market, with little recognition of skills and prior training. Some resist, but many accept that their dreams of what Canada might offer are just that — dreams. Adapting to these realities can mean reducing expectations and just surviving with what a job has to offer.

Transgressive learning is learning that can be generative of resistance. What are the conditions that lead to action? What kinds of social relations, contexts and circumstances help people move from learning only to adapt, to learning that supports resistance? There are several factors that are pertinent to a discussion of the development of this kind of learning. One important dimension involves deliberately working to build collective forms of action and consciousness. As our research shows, reconstituting social and political relations, through institutions such as community organizations or religious associations such as churches, appears to be central to this process. Again, as our research reveals, for most immigrants, it is clear that Canadian society is not welcoming and that immigrant groups, before they can become established, have to overcome a plethora of barriers and obstacles that continue to disrupt their lives many years after arriving in Canada. Challenging these as individuals often leads to very limited gains; whereas, for a minority it appears that building collective forms of solidarity, through both formal and informal means, acts as a powerful counterweight to the exploitative working environments in which they find themselves. Whether this solidarity arises through contact with a community organization such as the Immigrant Workers' Centre or a local church, workers who have experienced it appear to actively engage in forms of resistance and transgressive learning that raise critical questions concerning the relationship of immigrants to Canadian society. Some examples follow.

Sources of Support

In exploring the sources of support that allowed people to exercise different forms of workplace resistance, we found that they were quite varied: co-workers and unions, community groups, churches, family, friends, sympathetic workers in government institutions, even politicians! For some workers, it was a rich combination. Rosa, for example, attributed her confidence and willingness to assert herself and stand up for her rights to her "big mouth": she said she learned this assertiveness from her mother. Her co-workers taught her about her rights under the Labour Code, and people in her community (Filipino), the Immigrant Workers' Centre (IWC) and Kabataang Montreal (a Filipino youth group) helped her to see her personal situation as part of a larger political reality:

> Now, because of the help of others, they gave me courage to stand up for my rights.

Another interview participant, José, said that his main social network is within his church — a very close-knit community of Latinos from across Latin America. Members of the church provide emotional and financial assistance to one another in times of need. In the workplace, however, being able to distinguish between friends and foes, and building on the friendship of others was highlighted as important by a farmworker:

> Solidarity between workers [is key]. Here one finds friends who are good people for us. What happens is that we usually have to keep our mouths shut because there are people among the agricultural workers who, if you complain about the job, they go immediately to the overseer who knows how to speak Spanish.

Taking the time to find such allies from those of the same country of origin was really emphasized by workers as essential to their sense of comfort and well-being as they navigated their new context in Canada. This woman shares how her base of support when she first arrived made all the difference in terms of her long-term ability to withstand difficult times that came in the future:

> When we met, we would talk about the country, St. Kitts… We would go on picnics and we would go to each other's houses for parties to eat good food… It was good. That is why now I am able to stand a lot of what I am going through, because I had good times. But if I would have come to Canada and had bad times, I wouldn't be able to stand anything I'm going through now.

For most people, family was the starting point for support: spouses, children and more distant relatives all played a role in helping people to debrief difficult situations, to seek information and to take action. The following is an interesting example of a mother standing up for her daughter around employment issues, making good use of the threat of media exposure to further her point:

> My daughter… applied for a job as a director at the bank and originally she got the job but then they changed their mind… The person who gave her the job got orders from a more superior boss that the job was really meant for someone else. When my daughter called me, I told her that her job was really for her and that it was her job, but it was taken away from her. I called the bank and spoke to someone and I challenged their decision. I threatened the woman to come up with a good reason to explain why my daughter didn't get the job because otherwise, I was going to call the media. The bank called my daughter forty-five minutes later and sent her to work.

Given all the problems migrants shared with us regarding their access to social rights through government institutions and related tribunal and programs, it is very important to bring out the fact that, when workers encounter sympathetic individuals within these service centres (at the Labour Standards or Human Rights Commission, for example), it can make all the difference:

> It was a good experience [at the Labour Standards Commission] because the lady I had, explained certain things to me. She explained that, because we had a union, it limited me to a certain number of rights but that if I could prove that she was really, really prejudiced [then there were other places that could help]. So she gave me lots of information, like this lawyer I could call to find out what I could do. I called the lawyers and, you know, [it was really helpful].

To define resistance, we draw on the work of James Scott. He states: "Class resistance includes any act(s) by member(s) of a subordinate class that is or are intended to mitigate or deny claims made on that class by superordinate classes or to advance its own claims" (Scott 1985: 290). This definition is useful because it focuses on acts rather than on what is said, and it acknowledges that resistance is in a relationship of differing interests and power. Bayat comments that this position stresses that power and counter-power are not in binary opposition, but decoupled and complex — a perpetual "dance of control." Further, he states: "The resistance paradigm helps to uncover the complexity of power relations in society in general, and the politics of the subaltern in particular" (1998: 542). One cannot expect to find a universalized form of struggle. People resist by using those tools and opportunities to which they have access. In our interviews, we discussed the use of institutions such as government agencies — labour, health and safety standards — rather than day-to-day subversion that can occur directly in the labour process. Bayat raises the issue of large-scale versus individual acts and distinguishes between "real resistance," which is organized, systematic and preplanned, versus token resistance — unorganized, incidental acts without revolutionary consequences. He cites Brown's three forms of politics: 1) atomistic — the politics of individuals and small groups, which obscure content; 2) communal — a group effort to disrupt the system; 3) revolt — action taken to negate the system. In our interviews we find the acts associated with 1) and 2) to be present. A final comment by Bayat alerts us to the limits of the resistance paradigm:

> Acts of resistance, cherished so dearly, float around aimlessly in an unknown, uncertain and ambivalent universe of power relations, with the end result of an unsettled and tense accommodation with the existing power arrangements. (2000: 544)

Given the challenges in this analysis, it is important to raise several points. The first is the connection between resistance and the social context in which it arises. The social context is a key element in understanding the barriers to collective action. As we have already shown, these contextual issues have a determining impact on the "making of immigrant workers." We have also noted in our study the key role of the state in shaping contextual factors through policies, such as the LCP and SAWP, that limit the possibilities of resistance. In particular, the modern liberal state fragments, dissipates and ultimately limits potential threats of collective action through these policies, by deliberately endorsing individual challenges to violations of Labour Codes. Thus, while collective action is open for groups of workers to pursue through arbitration and other legal means, such action is inherently more complex and difficult to organize in cases of unjust dismissal. Another limiting force is the fragmentation of the contemporary labour market. In the Fordist period (c.1945–1980), large factories acted to bring workers together in a relatively stable working environment. However, with the demise of the Fordist regime of accumulation and its gradual replacement by neoliberalism from the 1980s, industrial production has become increasingly fragmented: thus workers are subject to more precarious working conditions, with the emergence of highly segmented labour markets. As a consequence, it has become more difficult to build the forms of collective consciousness in the workplace required for Brown's second category — communal resistance. Under these conditions, local community organizations such as the IWC come to play a key role in organizing and facilitating collective forms of action across a broad spectrum of issues by immigrant workers who often find themselves in atomized and poorly paid working environments.

Adapting to Limited Possibilities

This section is drawn from interviews we carried out with immigrant workers. We begin with a summary of the experience of a group of workers from Latin America, who have been in Canada for a period of fifteen to twenty-five years. These interviews told of an adaptive process, despite feelings of "lost hope." They express their adaptation to circumstances in which their skills and abilities have not been recognized, and their responses to their situation. In contrast with the stories of people who have resisted, we recount their stories of how they were able to do this and what happened to them in the process. Some of these are written as vignettes of their story; other specific experiences are cited to illustrate other points.

Between 1976 and 1986, a wave of Latin Americans came to Canada in search of political asylum. They came out of political necessity, fleeing repressive regimes that took away civil rights and their right to actively participate in their societies. These Latin American immigrants had been involved in political activity before coming to Canada. Their politics were established in the barrios and church activities in their homelands where they understood and struggled for social transformation and liberation.

We interviewed eighteen Latin American immigrants who had left their homeland because of fear of reprisals: they came to Canada in search of a better and more secure life. Almost half of them were political revolutionaries who had escaped from the dictatorial government of Chile, or from other regimes in Colombia and Peru. In the interviews, they talked of the democratic values of freedom of speech and the freedom to participate in non-violent demonstrations. Although they have strong commitments to integration into Canadian economic and social life, they also spoke of political activities to fight against social injustice. While most were firm in these beliefs, their integration into the political life of Canada became more difficult after their first few years. At first, most of them participated in the movement for the liberation of Chile by actively becoming involved in grassroots community organizations, such as those raising funds for political parties and creating support networks among Chilean and Colombian newcomers. They were involved in volunteer activities and eager to become agents of change in the politics of their country. But they did not participate in long-term political activity in the communities in Montreal. What are the barriers to such participation and more general integration in Canadian society? Political participation is not isolated from economic and social realities. In the interviews, they spoke about many barriers that contribute to their lack of participation in political life. These barriers have hindered their lives. Beginning a new life is not easy. They had to learn and negotiate basic elements of personal survival. Work was central in an increasingly competitive job market. The majority of the participants had post-secondary education with some technical degrees; half the participants had some university education. However, in spite of being well-educated and well-equipped for professional jobs, all of them, except for one, did not work in their professions. For the most part they work in low-wage service jobs as cleaners, hotel managers, janitors, taxi drivers and caretakers or as technicians of various sorts. Many of them started working in low-paying jobs, where they have been working for fifteen years or more. These low-paying jobs in the service sector draw on immigrants, who do not have officially recognized degrees, forcing them into situations of underemployment.

Another barrier to participation was language. They could all speak and communicate in French but stated that it was still difficult to articulate their experiences and give meaning to more profound expressions of emotions that are deeply rooted in their own language. This aspect is of special importance since the ability to participate fully in their wider community in Quebec is limited by language. Ironically, as this barrier did not permit total integration, it left them with superficial levels of communication. In reflecting on these barriers, the Latin American immigrants felt that they were caught in a constant process of negotiation and indecision over participation. In Quebec and the rest of Canada, the dominant belief is that new immigrants adapt through work and public life. However, long-term underemployment and little support for broader social and political participation were the experiences of this group of participants in our study. These immigrants have attempted to seek alternatives for a better life: yet, through their struggles, they have had constraints (work and language barriers) that have served to limit their political and social aspirations to surviving and "getting by," thus living without the capacity for broader political and social participation.

We can look at the examples of the interviews of the Latin Americans presented above and ask, what did people give up? What were the trade-offs? Many of them came with a politically active background but gradually gave it up to settle for dead-end jobs without hope of improvement. Similarly, the interviews with farm or domestic workers point to the huge stakes for individuals and to their lack of options. All of these factors act to maintain labour discipline and minimize opposition. Learning, in these circumstances, is principally concerned with how people analyze their situation and learn what is necessary for survival. This is why we have used the term, "learning in reverse," as a way of explaining and capturing the apparently compliant behaviour of people who labour under exploitative and often brutal conditions, but yet do not protest. Language was also an issue: although respondents possessed a functional understanding and an ability to communicate at work, they lacked a deeper capacity, which made it harder to participate in the wider society. The above examples demonstrate how everyday life, with the demands of work and family, and with little hope of recognition of education, skill and previous experiences, can lead people to resignation, even though they recognize the inherent injustices in this process.

Fighting Back and Resistance

As part of the research project reported in this book, we interviewed individuals who had some connection to the IWC. Significantly, they had all engaged in various forms of workplace resistance. However, while others that we interviewed were conscious of maltreatment, expressed resentment and were generally upset at being treated badly, the pressures they felt as immigrant workers to adapt were overwhelming. In the face of such pressures, we felt it was nevertheless remarkable that some people did take risks and challenge their employers. Clearly, there is a lot at stake, a lot to lose and very little in the way of political and social protection. The forms of resistance tended to be individual, for example, contesting work conditions at the Labour Standards office. The nature of the workplaces and the conditions of work were also not conducive to mass movements like strikes, picketing or other forms of collective mobilization. However, collective action was present in the context of the organizations that supported workers in contesting their situations. These include the IWC, PINAY (a Filipina organization that works with women in the LCP), and the Centre d'appui pour les travailleurs et travailleuses agricoles migrants du Quebec, which supports agricultural workers through specific campaigns.

The following vignette tells the story of one woman who learned to engage in workplace resistance in response to what she perceived as unfair and arbitrary behaviour on the part of management. Above all else, as she makes clear, the key issue for her was one of being treated with respect as a human being.

Maria

Maria is fifty-five years old, was born in El Salvador and has been in Canada since 1982 (twenty-four years). She is married, has three adult children and seven grandchildren. She is currently employed at Zellers in Montreal and stocks shelves. She earns $8.30/hour for thirty-five hours a week and works nights. Her job that immediately preceded this one was at Lamour, where she folded socks, earning $17,000/year (forty hours a week for $8.10/hour).

Migration Story

In El Salvador, Maria had been trained as a secretary in a post-secondary course and worked in her field. Her main social network there was provided by her church. When she became pregnant, she stopped work and stayed at home. She left her country because of the hardship of the war there and because her husband's cousin was targeted for political reasons. She and her family came to Canada as refugees. They applied to come to Canada in Mexico, where she worked as a domestic and her husband worked in construction. In Mexico, she was part of a group of Central Americans that provided mutual aid. Through that group, she received information about Canada and decided to apply to immigrate. She was accepted and arrived here with her husband and three children.

Working in Canada

When she arrived, she was counselled to take a French course, which she did. With three children, she was not able to return to school: thus she was never able to use her training in Canada. Her first job here was as a domestic worker. She found that job by chance through a friend, who was buying a car and talked to the salesperson, who was looking for a Spanish-speaking domestic. She worked there for three years. Her hours were from 8 a.m. to 10 p.m. She was paid by the hour and earned approximately $100–$120 a week.

Maria found her next job through her neighbour, a Spanish-speaking woman from Guatemala. Her employer was looking for workers. It was a job in manufacturing. The hours were from 8:30 a.m. to 4:30 p.m.: she received approximately $4/hour. The task she had was to fold bags after taking them from a machine. She had good relations with the other, mainly Spanish-speaking, employees (and with a few workers from Haiti). The boss was from Alberta. While in that job, she found out from another Spanish speaking worker that they were entitled to fifteen-minute coffee breaks. She pushed for this with her boss: they compromised with a ten-minute break. No one else supported her in the discussion. After four years in the job, the emissions from the plastic irritated her eyes to the point of forcing her to quit work. She did not receive CSST (occupational health) or unemployment benefits.

Maria began another search for work. This time she found a job through the "Help Wanted" section in a newspaper. The job was in the manufacturing sector and involved decorating boxes for Christmas. The work was initially full-time but when there was reduced demand, it became irregular. Maria needed full-time work and left the job. When asked about how she learned about her rights in the workplace, she said that she found out through friends, although she didn't have many. However, at the core of what she considered to constitute a good workplace was that it had to be a place where she would be respected as a person. Her next job was in the same company where her husband worked — L'Amour. It manufactured socks. Her husband worked on a machine and she folded socks. Her hours were from 7 a.m. to 5 p.m. No training for workers was provided. There were workers from all over the world. The largest group was from Sri Lanka, with a few from Latin America and India. When she arrived, one worker showed her what to do and she had to quickly make her quota. She stayed there for thirteen years.

At first there was some flexibility in the job and the production level was high. Unionization was initiated by a couple of people from Sri Lanka. One of the complaints that provoked the call included no eating tables for lunch (people ate at their machines). Although the organization of this workplace was not initiated by a union, nonetheless a union was formed. In her perception, the union was imposed: it appeared to be a "bosses' union." With the advent of the union, work became more tightly controlled. There was increased checking of the work done, through the use of tickets with employee numbers on them. There was less production, less talking and more stress. In general, there was more control of production: written notices were given if quotas were down. As Maria perceived it, there was close collaboration between the union and the company's human resources (HR) personnel.

Eventually Maria received notice that her performance was not satisfactory. HR told her that she was not fast enough. The company reduced her work hours. She signed a complaint in protest, but was sent home. She felt that this was because she knew her rights and because the supervisor did not like Latinos. Ultimately the pressure on her increased: finally, she was fired. Maria explained that prior to being fired, she was summoned to the HR office with three other women. The other three were crying and upset because the boss was complaining about inadequate production, asking, "Do you think I can pay for this lack of production?" Maria felt that the workers were being treated without respect. She told the women in charge of HR to stop harassing the workers. They wanted her to sign a document that she was in agreement with their evaluation. She refused because she knew it was in violation of labour standards (she had learned this from her son-in-law and from the IWC). She knew her rights, and the supervisor knew this. She was also not afraid because she had taken a course in HR as part of her training in El Salvador. She took this stance and spoke out because she believed that workers deserve respect from employers. There was a second meeting with HR, where they tried to convince her that she was a "bad worker" by showing her work not properly done, and claiming it was hers. She responded that it was not hers, that not everyone makes quotas and that she was being targeted and harassed.

Making a Complaint

Maria said that she made a complaint because she had spent many years working for the company, had met production targets, but was now receiving negative evaluations because she was challenging the authority of supervisors. After being fired, she found out about contesting her dismissal through the Immigrant Workers' Centre. She found out about the IWC through a pamphlet distributed through the organization's outreach program. Someone was giving out pamphlets at her workplace, but no one was taking them because of the presence of the security guard — people were afraid that they would lose their jobs. Nevertheless, she took the pamphlet while in a car and read it. She called the Centre and received help in Spanish.

Maria made her complaint at Normes de travail (Labour Standards) with the help of the IWC (the union discouraged her from complaining, saying it would not make a difference). She won her case: because she had not been given eight weeks' notice, she received compensation. Significantly, some recurrent health issues that had plagued her while working in the company (feeling stressed, difficulty sleeping, problems with vision and stomach irritations) went away at this point, so that she is now in better health. Her husband, who still worked for the company, noted that there were many improvements in working conditions after Maria filed her complaint at a tribunal. However, as there had been many layoffs, it was clear that the company had plans to close and relocate. In retrospect,

Maria felt that there were many workers like her being fired for not meeting quotas, or being harassed over performance issues, because the company wanted to get rid of as many people as it could before it closed, thus avoiding paying out severance packages. Maria reflected that, "If I am experiencing this kind of exploitation in the workplace and I do nothing about it, what will happen? So, I work for change, to give warning to these companies not to do it again."

As we have noted above, an important factor underlying individual actions was the demand that people had to be treated with respect. This was a theme that ran through the interviews we conducted. Below is one example of how the desire to be respected manifested itself in the workplace, when some new workers arrived from the Philippines:

> The floor lady started on me because I was the one who helped the new people when they came. And she loved treating the new people badly. There were some new people, Filipinos, and I had told them to come there to the job, and she treated them so badly so I felt bad. She started to give me more work, but my average was going down, so I asked her why my average went down when I was working more. She didn't like me talking to her like that, she doesn't like when people talk back to her. I went to the human rights association.

Demanding respect was at the core of this resistance. Here is another example of how the demand for respect generates resistance.

> But in general, I started watching all these relationships, this behaviour; when the supervisor started yelling at me, I told him, "Listen, I don't need a university degree to do this job — anyone can do this job, so you don't respect me, I don't respect you." So I tried to demand some respect as a worker, as a human being.

Mandel uses the concept of dignity in the same way we use respect. He argues:

> Dignity is a good starting point. A worker who respects his or herself may not be in a position to throw off oppression but he or she will at least not internalize it…. The awakened sense of dignity was (in the context of the [Russian] revolution of 1917), in turn, linked to social activism. (2004: 272)

Despite these individual acts of resistance, a number of interviewees acknowledged that some of their co-workers didn't take action because they feared their bosses. Aside from intimidation from employers and line supervisors, there is a lot at stake in taking action to either defend or promote one's workplace rights and material conditions. As we have seen, income for themselves and their families (in Canada and in their home country through remittances) is vital. So too is the time needed to participate in organizing efforts, when a typical working day may be ten or twelve hours long and when women feel obligated to do their domestic chores in addition to their factory work. Two workers most vividly expressed these limitations in the following way:

> A lot of Filipinos and others are silent in their jobs… They don't say anything in their jobs, even if they are exploited, because they are scared. They are scared that if they do something for change, they will be deported, especially those who are in the Live-In Caregiver Program, and even those with immigrant status. They are scared to be terminated. They feel held at the blade between life and death. Most of these people are closed, so it's better to go to the young people, because they are still motivated, receptive, but these people, forget about them — they are traditional, their mentality.

> Yes, they always want you to come to the meetings, they nudge you to come. But it's hard because, as I said, the system is so demanding — people don't have time to go to meetings after working hours, which are already so long. Also because garments and textiles are comprised of mostly women, they have responsibilities at home, so they aren't going to want to come to meetings; and even for men, it's hard to go spend two hours there.

For those new to Canada, finding out about basic rights, and then acting on that information to defend themselves in the workplace, is a huge challenge. For most people, there were connections to other individuals, unions and community organizations that played a key role. Some of these connections were informal, but initiative was required to make the connection, and then to act on the information that they received. The process of creating networks was a first step in getting information that could be used to resist in the workplace. Unions played a crucial role for many: for a couple of interviewees, unions became a means of earning a livelihood and of broadening their commitment to justice for immigrant workers. However, as Maria's story (above) indicates, the role of unions in supporting the immigrant workers is not always unambiguously to promote the interests and rights of workers they represented. As the quote from a textile worker below makes clear, unions must continuously be engaged in labour education with their members in order to be effective, as well as to ensure that they do not just reproduce the relations of capitalism with slightly improved conditions. Some workers commented on this as follows:

> I like to have the unions in the companies. But some of them are just following the orders of the management; they don't really fight for the workers. But still, I prefer to have unions because that will protect us. But this union will depend only on the members; if the members are updated and aware of their rights, they have options. If the members are not aware and educated, you could do something about it, to establish their own independence.

> I experienced union people discouraging workers, telling workers not to go for a case and fight for their rights, telling them that they wouldn't really have a chance at winning, but it was because it cost a lot of money to pursue it. But of course they don't say that it's because it costs a lot of money. The workers, they start to call back and complain. This is not providing a good education to the workers. Some unions are not really interested in providing this education.

In addition to unions, connections with community associations act as a way for new arrivals to connect with others and build relations of solidarity. For one person, her local community garden became a site for making meaningful connections:

> The community garden was my *famille d'accueil* (the family that welcomed me) here in Quebec. Without that, I would have been completely marginalized… I learned so much… about how to adapt — it was a place where I met friends… who told me how to get by without any money, where to buy cheap furniture…. They're now people I spend Christmas with.

For others, community organizations provided the means to engage politically, including supporting others in similar situations. One person to whom we talked had become very active in supporting non-status immigrants. Every week he visited a Palestinian family that had taken refuge in a church for over a year. As he said, "I go there… What can I do?… I help many people." He also attended weekly meetings of a support committee for Palestinian refugees where decisions were made about future actions, such as a march to Ottawa organized by Solidarity Across Borders, to demand the regularization of all refugees.

Everyday social relationships between people are the beginning point for learning and promoting individual and collective rights. For many workers to whom we talked groups like PINAY and the IWC have been more than a social network: they have made them aware of their rights as citizens and workers. Through their participation and involvement in these organizations, they have become politicized. As one person put it,

> I became more aware of things — and that changed everything for me here. I began going to all these meetings — basically everywhere my aunt told me to go, I would go. I started learning things like how the U.S. bought the Philippines from Spain. It changed the way I saw things — everything. You come here and you want to buy clothes at stores like the Gap, but then you go there and you look at the labels and you see it's made in the Philippines!

Significantly, these relationships were critical in transforming resentment into forms of action and resistance that gave new meaning and direction to the lives of those involved with the IWC. On meeting one of the IWC's organizers, a worker noted:

> I had filed the complaint already and then I met x on the street in front of the metro and I was encouraged. I just encountered x and she told me about (the IWC). I think I had heard of x before, somebody told me that x was with the Centre. When I looked at her, we were smiling and then we talked a long time. The centre helped me to call the union lawyer and ask them to do something.

Fine (2006), in her book on the emergence of community-based labour organizing, notes the importance for organizing immigrant labour of group formation and solidarity, arising either out of shared ethnicity or shared neighbourhoods. The IWC encompasses both, because of its location in an immigrant neighbourhood and its outreach to many different immigrant populations. The key element is to reach immigrant workers and provide a safe place for them where they can talk about and learn to act on work-related grievances. As the interviews indicated, a key element for building solidarity and collective action is the process of building relations not only with the staff of the Centre, but also, in the longer term and far more important, between immigrant workers themselves.

In terms of sources of support, our research suggests that it is very useful to tap into existing social networks. LCP workers were mainly Filipino; SAWP workers were from easily identified countries of origin (Mexico, Guatemala, Jamaica, for example) and were concentrated on farms. This made them easy to find. But in general, immigrant workers can be from anywhere in the world, arrive in small groups and may not be living in the community. Finding these workers is a major challenge: community social networks and information from Canadian workers will be key.

Our research also suggests that it is important to go beyond the workplace to forge alliances and relationships of trust with religious and ethnic associations. These groups, although they rarely have a labour rights vocation, are likely landing places for new arrivals looking for social activities and support from a familiar group. Progressive unions are another important ally. Unionized workers, in settings such as hotels, hospitals and resource extraction, work alongside immigrant workers, who may be hired on contract or as temporary workers. Educating union members to feel a sense of solidarity with immigrants, rather than feeling threatened by them, could go a long way toward the realization of their labour rights. It is important to build a sense of collective class consciousness regardless of background and status at work. Employers are experts at divide and rule, and use immigrants — both permanent and temporary workers — for short-term contracts. Building alliances and relationships, and demonstrating common interests is a key step in challenging employers.

Our exploration of the modes of action employed by immigrant workers (covert and overt individual and collective action) also taught us important lessons. For people under the type of pressures experienced by immigrant workers (necessity of sending remittances to the home country, competition for jobs, the desire to become permanent, often uncertainty about their status), covert resistance may be the most accessible form of struggle. Covert initiatives to maintain dignity and fight back must be acknowledged and valued as central to people's efforts to protect their self-esteem while protecting their jobs and their immigration status. In most cases where people take action around workplace conditions, we saw that personal interest was the first step towards collective action for the rights of many. From this perspective, providing individual advocacy can be seen as a way for workers to plug into something larger. A worker who has had success in demanding overtime pay, for example, may feel more confident in trying to mobilize co-workers to do the same. Individual advocacy cases are also rich sources of information on policy issues that merit campaigns. The extreme precarity of this workforce is another consideration to take into account. When the stakes of employment are so high, immigrant workers are likely to be highly distrustful of organizers and unwilling to take any risks to defend their rights. A related issue is that most of the organizing issues facing them will require long-term engagement, while their situation is defined by short-term visas.

Another group that is increasingly significant in Canada are those without legal status. They come here seeking refuge from a variety of situations as tourists or students and decide to extend their stay. This group is the most vulnerable in the labour market: they are forced to work under the table, and they do not have the same rights, as inadequate as they are, as other workers in Canada. The following vignette shows how an immigrant worker brought an articulate political analysis to his situation.

Omar

Migration

As a Palestinian refugee in Lebanon Omar had little future. He knew that despite his two years in university and his secondary diploma he would be limited to a job in one of the seventy-four chosen professions that Palestinians are allowed to pursue and that pay would be very limited. Canada, with its international reputation as peaceful and respectful of human rights, seemed a good destination. After obtaining a student visa for the U.S., he made his way to Canada hoping to continue his life.

> My target was coming to Canada, because I wanted to have a peaceful life. I know about Canada, about the regulations that you accept refugees, about the humanitarian whatever. She [Canada] has a reputation — a good reputation about that. So I say I want to start my life normal and peaceful. I would study and have a good job after and have a normal life.

Canada has not lived up to his expectations.

Immigration

His experience with the immigration system was drawn out and horrible.

> When I got to a lawyer she told me… I think she told me the truth. She told me, 'Look, I will be frank with you. In the IRB [Immigration and Refugee Board] you have two groups — two schools of judges — if you go to a judge from this school, 100 percent you get accepted. If you get a judge from this school, 100 percent you're rejected.' And that is what happened… after that, they started rejecting most of them. After that, I don't know anyone who was accepted — because some people, they are racist or something. Maybe it's because they don't drink coffee in the morning and they are in a bad mood and they go to work and they judge on someone's life and maybe this person, they end up losing five or six years of their life because they don't drink coffee. So if I get my papers, I think I'll distribute coffee to all the judges!

Omar was unlucky enough to get two judges that fell into the latter camp. He has friends from the same refugee camp in Lebanon, coming from similar situations who were accepted as refugees. Omar had his appeal rejected, received a deportation order and was living underground at the time of the interview.

Work

Since he arrived here close to five years ago, Omar has been working under the table. He has worked in a variety of jobs in the service sector: in bakeries, in produce, in distribution. He has worked as a bus boy, as a cook and in factories. His being "illegal" makes working difficult. He doesn't stay in a job for too long, out of fear he will be recognized and discovered by authorities. As a result he moves from job to job. He has lost track of the number of jobs he's had.

> I can't stay at the same place because of my status. I'm living underground. And there's a lot of people who know who you are and where you work so you have to leave because maybe they call Immigration. It depends. Some people you trust so it's OK, but some people you can't trust them, so you have to change. It's not good to stay in one place.

Fear of discovery is not the only reason he changes jobs periodically. Like other illegal workers here in Quebec, he feels he must put up with working conditions that other workers do not. His capacity to stand up for his rights is limited. He knows that he has no security and only a support network of friends to rely on — his employers know this also. Employers know they can pay him less, give him less hours and tell him to do a variety of difficult and menial tasks. He has no choice — other than to move on to another job:

> I learned to accept what I have. If you say I want to work forty [hours] and he says you can only have thirty, I have to take it… after that I look to find a place where I can get more hours. It happens a lot. Sometimes work is up, sometimes it's down. When business is down, they cut your hours. Me, I can't say anything, because I know that after one week I have no money so I never leave a job like that — I have to find another one. It's like from here to here — if you stay one week without job, you spend all the money you have, after that it's finished.

Organizing/Challenging

Omar is aware of the rights he should have as a worker here in Canada. This is not something that he learned from the official immigration system — but rather from friends — both Palestinian and Canadian. Another very significant source of learning has been through a group, the Coalition of Palestinian Refugees.

> At a certain time all the Palestinians were starting to get rejected. There was a group of judges who never accepted Palestinians. Before, it was OK, but when the numbers started to increase in Montreal, in other provinces I think it is the same, now here there are a lot. Most of the guys are rejected. So they get the idea to make a group.

Omar has been a part of the coalition since the beginning:

> When something is not fair, unjust. When you feel someone is supporting you, you feel you have to go. Now I have someone to ask if I have a question about my papers; if immigration catches me I have someone to ask… It's a lot of support. For learning… now every time I go to a lawyer, everything to say I know it before. I have a lot of experience now.

Learning to Cope

This kind of learning stands in marked contradiction to another kind of learning he has experienced — the learning involved in going from being a young university student who dreams of a future and career, to being an illegal worker living hand to mouth and in fear of deportation:

> I used to… first I want to go to university to continue my studies from Lebanon. I was hoping to continue my studies. Then work in that field after. OK then, you say, this is a job for one month, it's OK, it's part of my future. But being stateless, it's just the feeling that you're being stuck in this job. You changed from someone who wanted to make a Ph.D., or whatever, or at least working in a bad job but with certain projects to do… have your own business, whatever. You're changing from someone who has a good job, security, insurance… you have the right to say, 'OK, I'm sick today, I can't go to work.' You change to someone who's working under the table. You could lose your job at any time, and even the money you get is just enough for food and shelter, that's it, and it's the minimum, I think. Every human being has the right to get shelter and the right to get his food. So you're working just for that. You have the feeling that you're changing into someone who — I won't say a slave — but it's just like that. You're obliged because if you don't, you're on the streets. It's like that. You're not stable, you have nothing.
>
> You change, I tell you, when you live underground. You change a lot, a lot, a lot. After you have a lot of stress, after you stop doing the things you enjoy, you stop enjoying a lot of things, like after a bit of time you're not moving your head, you're not able to think of anything, of the future, you can't think of tomorrow, you can't plan to have a car, a cell phone. What you think: OK I should get money this week to get food. That's it. After a bit of time your brain stops. After one, two, three years, your head's not working anymore, your brain's not working.
>
> At first maybe it's too much… you're too nervous or maybe you quit the job but after that you learn — like me at first on the job, I was nervous, I fight with my boss, after that what did I get? I had no money, I had to find another job. It's difficult to find other jobs. So with experience you learn: OK, it's me… I'm not a normal human… like a human, he should have something in his head. He should not have to accept that, he sees that you're missing something… OK, I'm not normal, I have to stay here, I have to accept that…. After a while, you learn to accept that you have no choice. You have no choice. After a while, you start to feel that you have something wrong. Not the others. So after that you stop thinking of that. You do whatever. I tell you, you have to cancel your brain.

There are many people in Omar's situation living in the shadows of Canadian society, doing "whatever" in order to survive. However, despite his position, he is willing to fight back, to build solidarity with others and to challenge the ongoing mistreatment he experiences here. Resistance can be born in the worst of situations; it comes out of a need for respect, for the recognition that everyone has for who they are. At the same time, living without status takes its toll, as the costs of adapting to it are not without deep personal consequences.

Concluding Comments

The central argument that we have made in this chapter is that the category of immigrant worker has undergone change and transformation over the last thirty to forty years. In contrast with the period prior to 1970, immigrant workers are now mostly people of colour, who come from poorer parts of the world and who tend to find themselves, for extended periods, at the bottom of the labour market, despite high levels of education. The restructuring of the labour market under neoliberalism since the 1980s has been a key element in defining employment opportunities for this group. Many immigrant workers live with poorly paid, precarious, flexible job conditions that require long hours and do not produce adequate wages to surpass Canadian poverty levels. Further, because these jobs do not tend to be unionized, immigrant workers have little power to negotiate their conditions of work.

The life paths of immigrant workers we interviewed revealed how, and in what ways, the category of immigrant worker is constructed through a combination of neoliberal globalization, state-sponsored social policies and labour market segmentation in Canada. Their stories of leaving their countries of origin, particularly those of recent immigrants, describe desperation, flights from poverty and political repression. Since Canada represents a relatively safe place, people cannot simply go back to their homeland despite the difficulties they confront at work. In addition, many have obligations at home in Canada, as well as in their home country, where large numbers of immigrants remit significant portions of their salary to extended family members. These commitments raise the stakes for these workers in taking risks such as confronting exploitative working conditions: they also create a form of labour discipline. Settlement in Canada has also involved learning to live with disappointment. Arriving with professionally relevant credentials that are not recognized and therefore useless, as well as being designated as low- or unskilled workers, is a constant theme in the stories of those with whom we talked. Today's immigrant workers are consigned to the lowest levels of the Canadian labour market: this reality is key to understanding how the category of immigrant worker is being constructed in the contemporary period.

Becoming an immigrant worker involves understanding that one cannot go home and that one has to accept limited conditions and choices imposed by the Canadian labour market. Learning to adapt to a life of low income, long hours and precarious employment opportunities often necessitates a form of learning in reverse, in order to get by and survive. For some, learning to resist has also been experienced. Typically this type of learning emerged, among the workers we interviewed, when they engaged in struggle and contestation over working conditions and rights, which they felt violated their sense of integrity and self-respect. Where this happened, learning about how to take action of some kind usually followed. Individuals that did eventually take action always did so with the support of others, who provided information and other resources to help them in a dispute with an employer. These others can be unions, community organizations or co-workers or friends with whom they have informal relation-ships. "Street smarts" and small victories are shared between people: this in turn encourages others to take action. Such learning most often grows out of pre-existing relations with other individuals, peers or friends. However, organiza-tions play a key role. People find them by word of mouth when they are seeking knowledge and support. Organizations like the IWC build on and contribute to solidarity learning (discussed below), and provide political education and skills training that are necessary in such situations. Similarly organizations like PINAY and the Centre d'appui play an important role in accompanying individuals who take action on their own behalf. In addition, they mount public campaigns, organizing on questions of government policy.

Learning is tied to the daily life of immigrant workers, particularly in adapt-ing to and resisting the relationships of work. Some of this learning is centred on the different realities of Canadian life, including language and customs, and new skills for work. As we have shown, however, for many, learning was focused on how to adapt — i.e., to survive, to live with disappointment, despair, low incomes and employment instability. Others learned to volunteer and build supportive social networks. Again, from the interviews, it was clear that there was little or no employer-supported workplace learning. As Marie notes in the above vignette, someone shows you what to do: you have to make your quota. The challenge is to learn to "work hard and stay employed," no matter how bad the jobs, to keep your expectations low and to take what is offered. Part of becoming an immigrant worker, therefore, is to unlearn a former identity and to "re-define the self" as an "updatable resource," not a "human being." Immigrant workers have to learn to live two lives in Canada. One is a life of fear of supervisors and bosses, in which one must be compliant and silent about one's rights, and in which one must accept the fact that possibilities for action and change for the better are limited, if not illusory. The other life involves learning that, although injustice exists, one can resist it by taking action, by demanding respect as a human being and by refusing to be treated as a mere "human resource."

The issue of redefinition of self is a key and complicated issue confronting many in this study. It is related to the shifting identities of immigrant workers: as immigrants with associations with others from their countries of origin; with other workers and the wider working class; as women, particularly as domestic workers. Building and shaping collective identity is important to redefining the self in this context: it can contribute to building solidarity. However, there has to be a space (not virtual) for this to happen, either informally or through associations such as community organizations or unions. This is key to building a strong, collective voice. However, as have noted, without the tenacity and self-respect of the immigrant workers we interviewed, building collectively for action is almost impossible, given the difficult working conditions they face.

Church et al. (2008), examining community-based organizations, identified three forms of learning: political/organizational, solidarity and redefinition of self. Political/organizational learning is the way that the main actors in community organizations come to understand how to operate and position themselves in relation to the government and funders, and how to carry forward their agenda for social justice. Solidarity learning takes place, not according to an explicit curriculum, but spontaneously and unpredictably through social interaction in situations that foster people's participation. Reshaping the definition of self — becoming an immigrant worker — is a form of learning in which individuals build new identities and rethink who they are in relation to wider social definitions. This last form of learning is of particular importance for the lives of immigrants as they face challenges in positioning themselves in relation to the host society. This re-shaping of the self, of re-presenting the self in everyday life, as we have seen, was fraught with tensions and ambiguities for the immigrant workers we interviewed. In particular, the stories they told revealed an ongoing tension between learning in reverse and learning to resist in the workplace. This tension between learning to "get by" or survive and learning to question, challenge and engage in resistance is a historical phenomenon that has characterized workplace industrial relations since the emergence of capitalism in the late eighteenth century. The fact that it defines the experiences of the immigrant workers we interviewed in this study reveals, if nothing else, the contemporary relevance of this historical relation between capital and labour in understanding work and everyday life under neoliberal capitalism.

Justice and Dignity

The human costs borne by immigrant workers, whether arriving on temporary work visas or with resident status, stretch beyond poor, sometimes abusive working conditions, economic exploitation, racialization and racism. In his compelling account of taxi drivers in New York City and the struggle of the New York Taxi Workers Alliance, Biju Mathew succinctly describes the tensions in which immigrant workers often find themselves:

> The immigrant worker communities are placed in a peculiar bind. As long as the structure of "one globalized body" away in the First World is kept in place, a large part of the rest of the family's class experience changes for the better. But the working immigrant "alone" in the First World leads a life that is significantly empty of the more enduring signifiers of a meaningful life — love, intimacy, emotional attachments, and the sensual. (2005: 173–74)

The different forms of isolation that both LCP and SAWP workers face within Canada — hidden inside private homes and stuck on farms in rural areas — add to their invisibility and vulnerability, and compound their isolation from their families for whom they sacrifice so much. Said a factory worker, originally from Guatemala,

> I saw a lot of arrogance in the factories. The people had to work hard almost for nothing. And people had no choice but to work in bad conditions because they had responsibilities in their home countries.

Immigrant workers in Canada, whether on temporary guest-worker schemes like SAWP, landed or non-status, have to contend with a climate of renewed suspicion, fear and xenophobia informed by harsh economic times, the racialized way in which Canada and "real" Canadians are constructed and the renewed centrality of security in policy.

Mathew points out the severity of the current climate for immigrant workers in the U.S.:

> In the last three decades, "globalization" has, ironically, depended on shoring up the borders between nation states, especially those between the Third World and the First. What is even more important to note is that since September 11, 2001, those borders have hardened more than ever before. As thousands of working class and poor immigrant men are plucked from their homes, detained, and deported without any semblance of due process, the immigrant's internal sense of incarceration intensifies. (2005: 152)

Canada's own immigration/security state apparatus continues to deport non-status people and to label, surveill or detain others on the pretext of security. Contrary to some commentators' claims, we do not live in a borderless world.

Local Struggles, Global Systems of Apartheid

> Talk about your rights and the next day you're not there! — Srinath, immigrant worker

The struggles of immigrant workers for justice and dignity in Canada, on the farms in rural Quebec and Ontario, British Columbia, Alberta, Saskatchewan, Manitoba, New Brunswick, Nova Scotia and Prince Edward Island, behind the doors of suburban homes, in the factories, in taxis and in many other visible and invisible locations, mirror struggles in many other societies, where classes of working people are categorized in a hierarchy according to immigration status, race, gender and class. But these struggles must also be contextualized in relation to contemporary social movement mobilization in an era of global capitalism and economic apartheids.

Union responses in the past to the struggles of migrant and new immigrant workers have sometimes been hostile or tepid. As Indian political economist Amiya Bagchi notes, "deliberate attempts have been made to incorporate the workers of the advanced capitalist countries in the imperialist project by portraying the workers of the developing countries rather than footloose capital as their enemies" (2005: 323). The erosion of trades jobs, attacks on unionism, policies of labour deregulation and changes to the nature and structure of work through flexibilization, casualization, subcontracting chains and relocation of industry to cheaper production sites have in some cases fuelled exclusionary or racist practices within unions towards new immigrants, rather than of solidarity and support for struggles for workplace justice and within the wider society. However, under pressure from their own membership, and from outside, some trade unions are now rethinking past practices and addressing challenges thrown up by migrant workers in the current face of neoliberalism.

In the face of these and other challenges, we have described different modes of labour organizing by immigrant workers through organizations such as the IWC, PINAY and the UFCW-supported Centre d'appui pour les travailleurs et travailleuses agricoles saisonniers. However, these groups do not work in isolation. They are connected with both the union movement and wider social movements, both locally based and international. The relationship with trade unions is complex. At times unions have been important allies, as the support given by them to the IWC and Centre d'Appui shows. Unions have supported campaigns initiated by the IWC and, in turn, the IWC has collaborated with a few union drives in specific workplaces. At other times, the IWC has contested the practices of some unions that have not adequately represented their members. The relationship is thus one formed in ambiguity. Unions need to be active in organizing new members: currently the most obvious group is constituted by immigrant workers. However, given the types of jobs held by many immigrants, and other barriers such as language and cultural differences, this is not an easy task. New models of organizing are required that link a community approach to traditional unionization and that use campaign strategies to bring about reforms that can improve the situations of immigrant and all low-wage workers in the contemporary economy.

Moreover, migrant worker struggles for justice in Canada must be seen in a global context. Around the world, migrant workers, established immigrant communities and, in some cases, second- and third-generation immigrant workers provide pools of "cheap" labour to be exploited by local and transnational economic interests: these cheap labour pools are pivotal to the functioning of many societies. On the other hand, as they have been throughout history, they provide convenient scapegoats for social, political and economic ills. In 2008, anti-immigrant violence flared up in a number of countries, including Italy, where vicious attacks were made on Roma camps in Naples and Milan; Romania, where hundreds of Romanians were detained in supposedly anti-street-crime operations; and in Italy again, where the prime minister, Silvio Berlusconi, promised to crack down on illegal immigration and to introduce mandatory fingerprinting for immigrants (Pisa 2008; Owen 2008). Violence in South Africa, directed largely against immigrants from Mozambique, Zimbabwe and other African countries, also made world headlines in 2008 (BBC News 2008). Meanwhile, struggles of migrant workers to organize for justice and dignity take place under intense state repression in countries as far apart as South Korea and the Gulf states. In May 2008, for example, two longtime migrant-worker organizers in Korea, Torna Limbu (from Nepal) and Abdus Sabur (from Bangladesh) were arrested, jailed, beaten and deported during a crackdown ordered by newly elected President Lee Myung-bak, who vowed to use force, if necessary, to expel foreign workers who were in Korea without the necessary papers (Asian Human Rights Commission 2008). Unions and other activists denounced this treatment and charged that the two had been targeted for their organizing work, as respective president and vice-president of the Migrants Trade Union in Korea. Over the summer of 2008, Kuwaiti authorities expelled over a thousand Bangladeshi workers who had gone on strike over unpaid wages and poor working conditions (Ahmed 2008).

However, migrant workers and their organizations are also mobilizing and joining forces at local, national and international levels too. There is a wider international movement for migrant justice, composed of immigrant workers and their allies. In Canada, too, there are groups and networks that work more broadly on issues of immigration status, such as No One Is Illegal (available at <http://nooneisillegal.org>) and Solidarity Across Borders (available at <http://www.solidarityacrossborders.org>), and on issues of racial profiling and security certificates, like the Justice Coalition for Adil Charkaoui (available at <http://www.adilinfo.org>). These groups and movements organize broader campaigns that mobilize across organizations and bring people together to challenge the general condition of migrants, as well as specific concerns. It is important to build beyond the local and connect on some of the wider conditions facing migrants. Internationally, new organizations have been founded to build solidarity, to share local experiences and to express the fact that the injustices faced by migrants worldwide are similar and are a result of the global displacement linked to neoliberal capitalism. In a situation in which countries like the Philippines export domestic workers around the world, international organizing provides a means for sharing knowledge and strategies, and building solidarity. The first step toward justice for immigrant workers begins with local organizing: carrying struggles further requires allies such as unions and wider social movements to challenge the power of international capital.

In Hong Kong in June 2008, an assembly of 118 migrant workers' organizations and their allies from twenty-five countries across the world, including a sizeable delegation from several cities in Canada (among them representatives from the Immigrant Workers' Centre and PINAY in Montreal), met to form the International Migrants Alliance (IMA) (available at <http://pinas.net/ima>). The Alliance aims to strengthen solidarity connections between migrant workers' struggles and to coordinate joint actions and campaigns on issues such as just wages, job security, criminalization of undocumented migrants and the trafficking of women.

More recently, the October 2008 intergovernmental Global Forum on Migration and Development (GFMD), hosted in Manila, Philippines, was challenged by migrant workers' and refugee organizations and their advocates who are organizing a counter-conference and mass action under the slogan: "Migrants' Challenge to the GFMD: End poverty, ensure jobs at home, stop forced migration! Uphold and Protect the rights of Migrants and Refugees!" (IAMR 2008). The organizers of this event strongly critique dominant positions on migration and development, contending that the GFMD promotes "greater commodification of migrants and the perpetuation of conditions for cheap labor, not to mention the social costs of migration, especially on children and families."

These movements charge that the dominant concept of "development" through migration and the reliance on remittances as development tools are neoliberal ideas and strategies which thrive

> on people's exploitation and miseries of migrants, enhances labor flexibilization and therefore, greater commodification of labor, and only brings Third World countries into the quagmire of poverty because these do not address the root causes of underdevelopment and the massive migration of peoples from poor countries. (IAMR 2008)

Global capitalism fragments labour and the lives of working people everywhere. The structured precarity of many migrant workers' immigration and employment status is one of the conveniently underdiscussed aspects of neoliberal economic development. To adapt a slogan used in a number of campaigns by migrant workers in Canada, one must ask that if workers are good enough to work are they also not good enough to stay? Immigrant worker struggles are some of the most significant movements in contemporary North America, with important implications for broader societal change. With reference to recent major mobilizations against neoliberal globalization and global capital, Vijay Prashad (2003) asks who is at the frontline of the struggles against capitalist globalization. Arguing for the importance of incremental struggles by the contingent class — predominantly people of colour and the working poor — and the disconnect between them and the majority of those who participate in major mobilizations of the "anti-globalization" movement, he notes that the question

> is not just about gaps that have opened up between those who demonstrate and those who don't, but between those who think they are at the frontlines when they toss the tear gas canisters back at the police and those who face routine political disenfranchisement, economic displacement, social disdain, and yet spend their days in their own forms of fight-back. (2003: 194)

Recently, immigrant workers' mobilizations and organizing in both the U.S. and Canada have attained a higher profile and in many ways represent perhaps the most vibrant social movement in those countries. As Verda Cook, author of the Canadian Labour Congress research report *Workers of Colour Within a Global Economy* argues,

> the migrant struggle for better conditions and Canadian residency is critical in holding the line against declining wages and working conditions for the entire labour movement. They are at the edge of the economic divide and must be protected and involved in our collective struggle in order for real change to occur. A worker is a worker is a worker. (2004: 5)

References

Abu-Laban, Y., and C. Gabriel. 2002. *Selling Diversity: Immigration, Multiculturalism, Employment Equity and Globalization*. Peterborough, ON: Broadview Press.

Ackerman, F., T. Wise, K. Gallagher, L. Ney and R. Flores. 2003. "Free Trade, Corn, and the Environment: Environmental Impacts of US–Mexico Corn Trade Under NAFTA." Global Development and Environment Institute. No. 03-06. Available at <http://ase.tufts.edu/gdae/Pubs/wp/03-06-NAFTACorn.PDF> accessed January12, 2008.

AFL (Alberta Federation of Labour). 2006. "AFL Policy Statement on Temporary Foreign Workers." Available at <http://www.afl.org/campaigns-issues/tempworker/statement.cfm> accessed May 22, 2008.

Ahmed, Hana Shams, 2008. "Sweatshop Tales." Daily Star (Dhaka), Star Weekend Magazine. August 29. Available at <http://www.thedailystar.net/magazine/2008/08/05/s_feature.htm> accessed September 17, 2008.

Arat-Koç, S. 1999. "Neo-liberalism, State Restructuring and Immigration: Changes in Canadian Policies in the 1990s." *Journal of Canadian Studies*, 34(2): 31–56.

Asian Human Rights Commission. South Korea. 2008. "Two Newly Elected Migrants' Union Leaders again Deported." May 19. Available at <www.ahrchk.net/ua/mainfile.php/2008/2860> accessed September 17, 2008.

Bagchi, A.K. 2005. *Perilous Passages. Mankind and the Global Ascendancy of Capital*. Lanham, MD: Rowman and Littlefield.

Baines, D., and N. Sharma. 2002. "Migrant Workers as Non-Citizens: The Case against Citizenship as a Social Policy Concept." *Studies in Political Economy* 69: 75–128.

Bakan, A.B., and D.K. Stasiulis. 1995. "Domestic Placement Agencies and the Racialization of Women's Domestic Work." *Signs* 20, 2 (Winter): 303–35.

Barber M. 1991. *Les domestiques immigrantes au Canada*. Ottawa, Société historique du Canada, Coll. Les Groupes ethniques du Canada (16): 33.

Basok, T. 2007. "Regulating Class Privilege: Immigrant Servants in Canada, 1940–1990s." *International Migration Review* 29(4): 21–25.

Bauder, H. 2003. "'Brain Abuse,' or the Devaluation of Immigrant Labour in Canada." *Antipode* 35, 4: 699–717.

Bayat, A. 2000. "From 'Dangerous Classes' to Quiet Rebels: Politics of Urban Subaltern in the Global South." *International Sociology* 15, 3 (September): 533–57.

BBC News. 2008. "S. Africa to set up Migrant Camps." May 28. Available at <*news.bbc.co.uk/1/hi/world/africa/7422887.stm*> accessed September 17, 2008.

Berger, J., and J. Mohr. 1975. *A Seventh Man*. London: Penguin.

Blackell, G. 2001. "Presentation on the UN Convention Against the Trafficking of Human Beings." Ottawa: National Metropolis Conference. October 19.

Blackett, Adelle. 2008. "International Law Related to Migrant Domestic Workers." Presentation to the Commission des droits de la personne et des droits des jeunes. Montreal, QC. June.

Bolaria, Singh B. 1990. "Health Status and Immigrant Status: Women and Racial Minority Workers." Madrid: International Sociological Association.

Boti, M., and F. Bautista. 1999. *When Strangers Meet*. Film produced by National Film Board Canada.

Bouchard-Taylor Consultation Commission on Accommodation Practices Related to Cultural Differences/Commission de consultation sur les practiques d'accommodement reliées aux differences culturelles. Available at <http://www.accommodements.qc.ca> accessed January 2009/

Brem, Maxwell. 2006. "Migrant Workers in Canada: A Review of the Canadian Seasonal Agricultural Workers Program." Ottawa: North-South Institute. Available at <http://www.nsi-ins.ca/english/publications/policy_briefs.asp> accessed March 2009.

Calliste, Agnes. 1991. "Canada's Immigration Policy and Domestics from the Caribbean: The Second Domestic Scheme." In J. Vorst et al. (ed.), *Race, Class, Gender: Bonds and Barriers*. 2nd ed. Toronto: Garamond Press.

Canada, House of Commons. 1984. *Equality Now! Report of the Special Committee on Participation of Visible Minorities in Canadian Society*. Ottawa.

Canadian Council for Refugees. 2005. "Ten Reasons Why Safe Third Country Is a Bad Deal." Available at <http://www.web.net/ccr/10reasons.html> accessed August 4, 2008.

Canadian Heritage. "Canadian Diversity: Respecting our Differences." Available at <http://www.pch.gc.ca/progs/multi/respect_e.cfm> accessed August 4, 2008.

CATTA (Coalition d'appui aux travailleurs et travailleuses agricole). 2004. "Report of 212 Documented Testimonies of Foreign Mexican and Guatemalan Agriculture Workers Registered in PTAT for the 2004 Season, Attached to 53 Farms in the Province of Quebec, Canada."

Caulford, P., and Y. Vali. 2006. "Providing Health Care to Medically Uninsured Immigrants and Refugees." *CMAJ* 194: 1253–54.

CBC. 2008. "Tories Survive Another Confidence Vote, MPs Vote in Favour of Bill C-50." Available at <http://www.cbc.ca/canada/story/2008/06/09/immigration-vote.html> accessed August 4, 2008.

CCNC (Chinese Canadian National Council) website <http://www.ccnc.ca/redress/history.html> accessed January 2009.

Chacón, J.A., and M. Davis, M. 2006. *No One Is Illegal: Fighting Racism And State Violence on the US-Mexico Border*. Chicago: Haymarket Books.

Chang, G. 2000. *Disposable Domestics: Immigrant Women Workers in the Global Factory*. Cambridge, MA: South End Press.

Chang, K., and L.H. Ling. 2000. "Globalization and Its Intimate Other: Filipina Domestic Workers in Hong Kong." In M.H. Marchand and A.S. Runyan (eds.), *Gender and Global Restructuring: Sightings, Sites and Resistances*. London: Routledge.

Chossudovsky, M. 1998. *La Mondialisation de la Pauvreté*. Montréal: Écosociété.

Choudry, A., G. Mahrouse and E. Shragge. 2008. "Neither Reasonable nor Accommodating." *Canadian Dimension* May-June: 16–18.

Church, K., J-M. Fontan, R. Ng and E. Shragge. 2000. *Social Learning among People Excluded from the Labour Market Part One: Context and Case Studies*. Toronto: NALL.

_____. 2008. "While No One is Watching: Learning in Social Action Among People who are Excluded from the Labour Market." In K. Church, N. Bascia and E. Shragge (eds.), *Learning through Community-Exploring Participatory Practices*. Netherlands: Springer.

CIC (Citizenship and Immigration Canada). 1999. "The Live-In Caregiver Program: Information for Employers and Live-In Caregivers from Abroad." Available at <http://www.cic.gc.ca/english/visit/caregi_e1.html> accessed February 2001.

_____. 2000. "Facts and Figures 1999 — Immigration Overview: Other Class by Principal Applicants by Gender, 1999." Available at <http://www.cic.gc.ca/english/pub/facts99/7other-02.html> accessed February 2001.

_____. 2007. "Facts and Figures 2006 — Immigration Overview: Permanent Residents by Top Source Countries." Available at <http://www.cic.gc.ca/english/resources/statistics/facts2006/permanent/12.asp>.

Coalition Justice for Adil Charkoui. Website. <http://www.adilinfo.org> accessed September 17, 2008.

Cohen, R. 2000. "Mom Is a Stranger: The Negative Impact of Immigration Policies on the Family Life of Filipina Domestic Workers." *Ethnic Studies* 32: 76–89.

Commission des normes du travail. 2001. *Labour Standards in Quebec and Domestics Residing with Their Employer*. Quebec: Gouvernement du Quebec.

Conference Board of Canada. 2004. *Making a Visible Difference: The Contributions of Visible Minorities to Canadian Economic Growth. Economic Performance and Trends*. April. Ottawa. Available at <http://www.conferenceboard.ca/documents.aspx?DID=705> accessed March 2009.

Cook, V. 2004. "Workers of Colour Within a Global Economy." Canadian Labour Congress. Available at <http://canadianlabour.ca/updir/research.pdf> accessed September 17, 2008.

Côté, A., M. Kérisit and M.-L. Côté. 2001. *Sponsorship… For Better or Worse: The Impact of Sponsorship on the Equality Rights of Immigrant Women*. Ottawa: Status of Women Canada.

Daenzer, P. 1993. *Regulating Class Privilege: Immigrant Servant in Canada, 1949s–1990s*. Toronto: Canadian Scholars' Press.

Diocson, C. 2001. "Filipino Women's Identity: A Social, Cultural and Economic Segregation in Canada." Available at <http://www.december18.net/paper18Ph-Canada.htm> accessed January 2009.

Edwards, N.C. 1994. "Translating Written Material for Community Health Research and Service Delivery: Guidelines to Enhance the Process." *Canadian Journal of Public Health* 1: 67–70.

Fairley, D., C. Hanson, G. Arlene, T. McLearen, G. Otero, K. Preibish and M. Thompson. 2008. "Cultivating Farmworker Rights: Ending the Exploitation of Immigrant and Migrant Farmworkers in B.C." Canadian Center for Policy Alternatives-B.C., Justicia for Migrant Workers, Progressive Intercultural Community Services, B.C. Federation of Labour. Available at <http://www.policyalternatives.ca/News/2008/06/farmworkers> accessed August 1, 2008.

FARMS (Foreign Agricultural Resource Management Services). 2003. *The Quest for a Reliable Workforce in the Horticulture Industry*. Mississauga: Foreign Agricultural Resource Management Services.

Ferrier, V. 2006. "The Square Tomato Capital of Canada. Leamington Ontario: 'The Best Place to Live' For Who?" *The Dominion* 26. Available at <www.dominionpaper.ca/agriculture/2006/05/25/the_square.html> accessed July 22, 2008.

Fine, J. 2006. *Worker Centers: Organizing Communities at the Edge of the Dream*. Cornell, NY: Cornell University Press.

Foley, G. 2001. "Emancipatory Organisational Learning: Context and Method." *Conference Proceedings from the Second International Conference on Researching Work and Learning*. Calgary, AB: Faculty of Continuing Education, University of Alberta.

Forum régional sur le développement social. 2007. *Quand le travail n'empêche plus être pauvre*. Montréal: Les suites, Conseil Régionale des Elus. Février.

Gibb, H. 2006. *Farmworkers from Afar: Summary Findings from the North-South Study on Canada's Seasonal Agricultural Workers Program as a Model of Best Practices in Migrant Worker Participation in the Benefits of Economic Globalization*. Ottawa: North-South Institute.

_____. 2007. "Temporary Foreign Worker Programs: Opportunities and Challenges." Workshop on Building Value in Temporary Migration Programs. SALISES (Sir Arthur Lewis Institute of Social and Economic Studies), UWI (University of West India) Cave Hill Campus, Barbados and SALISES, Mona Campus, Jamaica. The North-South Institute.

Gibson, A., E. Calugay and J. Hanley. 2008. "Reform of the Temporary Foreign Worker Program: Fundamental Changes Required." Proposal of Alternative Policies for Integration Programs for Foreign Workers in Canada for Submission to Citizenship and Immigration Canada and Human Resources and Social Development Canada. Montreal: Centre des travailleurs et travailleurs Immigrants/Immigrant Workers' Centre, PINAY, Droits des travailleuses et travailleurs (im)migrantes.

Gibson, N., A. Cave, D. Doering, L. Ortiz and P. Harms. 2005. "Socio-cultural Factors Influencing Prevention and Treatment of Tuberculosis in Immigrant and Aboriginal Communities in Canada." *Social Science and Medicine* 61: 931–42.

Global Forum on Migration and Development. Website. Available at <http://www.gfmd2008.org> accessed September 17, 2008.

Gravel S., L. Boucheron and M. Kane. 2003. "Workplace Health and Safety for Immigrant Workers in Montreal: Results of an Exploratory Study." *Perspectives interdisciplinaires sur le travail et la santé* 5.

Guatemala. 2008. "Segunda Evaluación Programa Trabajadores(as) Agrícolas Temporales Canadá." Available at <http://www.oim.org.gt/Cuaderno%20de %20Trabajo%20No.%2025.pdf> accessed July 22, 2008.

Guruge, S., and N. Khanlou. 2004. "Intersectionalities of Influence: Researching the Health of Immigrant and Refugee Women." *Canadian Journal of Nursing Research* 36: 32–47.

Handlin, O. 1951. *The Uprooted*. New York: Grosset and Dunlap.

Hanley, J., and E. Shragge. Forthcoming. "Economic Security for Women with Precarious Immigration Status: Enforcing Labour Rights for All." In J. Pulkingham and G.M. Cohen (eds.), *Imagining Public Policy to Meet Women's Economic Security Needs*. Ottawa: Canadian Centre for Policy Alternatives.

Hanley, W. 2007. *UFCW Canada Report on the Status of Migrant Farm Workers in Canada, 2006–2007*. Available at <http://www.ufcw.ca/Theme/UFCW/files/PDF2007/ StatusReportEN2007.pdf> accessed May 23, 2008.

Hart, M.U. 1992. *Working and Educating for Life-Feminist and International Perspectives on Adult Education*. London and New York: Routledge.

Hayter, T. 2000. *Open Borders: The Case Against Immigration Controls*. London: Pluto.

Hernàndez-Cos, R. 2005. "The U.S.-Mexico Remittance Corridor: Lessons on

Shifting from Informal to Formal Transfer Systems." World Bank Working Paper No. 47. Washington, D.C.: The World Bank. Available at <http://siteresources. worldbank.org/EXTAML/Resources/396511-1146581427871/US-Mexico_ Remittance_Corridor_WP.pdf> accessed August 8, 2008.

Hodge, J. 2006. "Unskilled Labour: Canada's Live-In Caregiver Program." *Undercurrent* 3: 60–66.

Human Resources and Social Development Canada. 2006. Temporary Foreign Worker Program Improved for Employers in B.C. and Alberta." Available at <http://news.gc.ca/web/view/en/index/jsp?articleid=350829> accessed August 4, 2008.

_____. 2008. "Agreement for the Employment in Canada of Commonwealth Caribbean Seasonal Agricultural Workers." Available at <http://www.hrsdc. gc.ca/eng/workplaceskills/foreign_workers/forms/carib2008cont-e.pdf> accessed March 2009.

Iacovetta, F., P. Draper and R. Ventresca (eds.). 1998. *A Nation of Immigrants: Women, Workers, and Communities in Canadian History, 1840s–1960s.* Toronto: University of Toronto Press.

IAMR (International Assembly of Migrants and Refugees). 2008. "Migrants' Challenge to the GFMD." concept paper. Available at <www.apmigrants. org/attachments/Concept_Paper_Migrants_Challenge_to_the_GFMD.doc> accessed September 17, 2008.

International Labour Organization. 2002. Current Dynamics of International Labour Migration: Globalisation and Regional Integration. Available at <http:// www.ilo.org/public/english/protection/migrant/about/index.htm> accessed January 5, 2009.

International Migrants Alliance. Website. <http://pinas.net/ima> accessed September 17, 2008.

Justicia4Migrant Workers. Website. <http://www.justicia4migrantworkers.org/saw. htm> accessed August 4, 2008.

Juteau, D. 1997. "Gendering Immigration/Integration Policy Research: Research Gaps." Proceedings of the Metropolis First National Conference on Immigration in Edmonton, AB, March 6–8, 1997. Available at <http://canada.metropolis. net/events/edmon/index_e.html> accessed January 2009.

Kamat, S., A. Mir and B. Mathew. 2004. "Producing Hi-tech: Globalization, the State and Migrant Subjects." *Globalisation, Societies and Education* 2, 1: 1–39.

Kapur, D. 2004. "Remittances: The New Development Mantra?" G-24 Discussion Paper, 29. Available at <http://www.unctad.org/Templates/Download.asp?do cid=4855□=1&intItemID=2103> accessed August 4, 2008.

Karas, Sergio R. 1997. "Canada: The Live-In Caregiver Program." Paper presented to the International Bar Association, Migration and Nationality Committee, New Delhi.

Kinsman, G., D.K. Buse and M. Steedman (eds.). 2000. *Whose National Security? Canadian State Surveillance and the Creation of Enemies.* Toronto: Between the Lines.

Kopec, J.A., J.I. Williams, T. To and P.C. Austin. 2001. "Cross-cultural Comparisons of Health Status in Canada Using the Health Utilities Index." *Ethnicity and Health* 6: 41–50.

Krane, J., J. Oxman-Martinez and K. Ducey. 2001. "Violence Against Women and

Ethnoracial Minority Women: Examining Assumptions about Ethnicity and Race." *Canadian Ethnic Studies* 32 (3): 1–18.

Krznaric, R. 2005. "The Limits on Pro-Poor Agricultural Trade in Guatemala: Land, Labour and Political Power." Occasional paper. UNDP Human Development Report Office. Available at <http://hdr.undp.org/en/reports/global/hdr2005/papers/hdr2005_krznaric_roman_17.pdf> accessed August 4, 2008.

Lai, D.W.L., and S.B.Y. Chau. 2007. "Predictors of Health Service Barriers for Older Chinese Immigrants in Canada." *Health and Social Work* 32: 57–66.

Langevin, L., and M.-C. Belleau. 2000. *Trafficking in Women: A Critical Analysis of the Legal Framework for the Hiring of Live-In Immigrant Domestic Workers and the Practice of Mail-Order Marriage*. Ottawa: Status of Women Canada.

Li, C., G. Gervais and A. Duval. 2006. "The Dynamics of Overqualification: Canada's Underemployed University Graduates." April. Ottawa: Statistics Canada. Catalogue no. 11-621-MIE2006039.

Lippel, K. 2006. "Precarious Employment and Occupational Health and Safety Regulation in Quebec." In L. Vosko (ed.), *Precarious Employment: Understanding Labour Market Insecurity in Canada*. Montreal-Kingston: McGill Queen's University Press.

Livingstone, D., and P. Sawchuk. 2000. "Beyond Cultural Capital Theory: Hidden Dimensions of Working Class Learning." Unpublished manuscript.

Macklin, A. 1992. "Foreign Domestic Worker: Surrogate Housewife or Mail Order Servant?" *McGill Law Journal* 37: 681.

Mahrouse, G. 2006. "(Re)Producing a Peaceful Canadian Citizenry: A Lesson on the Free Trade of the Americas Quebec City Summit Protests." *Canadian Journal of Education* 29, 2: 436–53.

Maitra, S., and H. Shan. 2007. "Transgressive Vs, Conformative: Immigrant Women Learning at Contingent Work." *Journal of Workplace Learning* 19, 5: 286–95.

Mandel, D. 2004. *Labour After Communism*. Montreal: Black Rose Books.

Mathew, B. 2005. *Taxi! Cabs and Capitalism in New York City*. New York: New Press.

McKay, D. 2003. "Filipinas in Canada — Deskilling as a Push toward Marriage." In N. Piper and M. Roces (eds.), *Wife or Worker? Asian Women and Migration*. Lanham: Rowman and Littlefield.

McNally, D. 2002. *Another World Is Possible: Globalization and Anti-Capitalism*. Winnipeg: Arbeiter Ring.

MICC (Ministère de l'immigration et des communautés culturelles). 2008. *Tableaux sur l'immigration au Quebec 2003–2007*. Quebec, PQ: MICC.

Mimeault, I., and M. Simard. 1999. "Exclusions légales et sociales des travailleurs agricoles saisonniers véhiculés quotidiennement au Quebec." *Relations Industrielles/Industrial Relations* 54, 2: 388–410.

Morin, A. 2007. "Syndicalisation des Travailleurs saisonniers: Les producteurs se détournent du Mexique." *La Presse* juillet 26.

National Farmers Union. 2005. "The Farm Crisis and Corporate Profits: A Report by Canada's National Farmers Union." Available at <www.nfu.ca/new/corporate_profits.pdf> accessed June 23, 2008.

Ng, Roxanna. 1992. "Managing Female Immigration: A Case of Institutional Sexism and Racism." *Canadian Woman Studies* 12, 3.

No One Is Illegal. Website. <http://nooneisillegal.org> accessed September 17,

2008.

Osborne, Margaret. 2001. "Bridging the Community and Accreditation System in the Removal of Barriers to the Recognition of Foreign Qualifications." Research in progress. Presented at National Metropolis Conference, Ottawa, October 17, 2001.

Owen, R., 2008. "EU clears Berlusconi over Roma Gypsies." *The Times*. September 4. Available at <http://www.timesonline.co.uk/tol/news/uk/article4674724. ece> accessed September 17, 2008.

Oxman-Martinez, J., J. Hanley and L. Cheung. 2004. *Another Look at the Live-In Caregiver Program*. Montréal: Immigration et métropoles.

Oxman-Martinez, J., J. Hanley, L. Lach, N. Khanlou, S. Weerasinghe and V. Agnew. 2005. "Intersection of Canadian Policy Parameters Affecting Women with Precarious Immigration Status: A Baseline for Understanding Barriers to Health." *Journal of Immigrant Health* 7: 247–58.

Oxman-Martinez, J., A. Martinez and J. Hanley. 2001. "Trafficking Women: Gendered Impacts of Canadian Immigration Policy." *Journal of International Migration and Integration* 2, 3: 297–313.

_____. 2001. "Human Trafficking: Canadian Government Policy and Practice." *Refuge* 19, 4: 14–23.

Parreñas, R. 2000. "Migrant Filipina Domestic Workers and the International Division of Reproductive Labour." *Gender and Society* 14, 4: 560–80.

_____. 2001a. "Mothering From a Distance: Emotions, Gender, and Intergeneration Relations in Filipino Transnational Families." *Feminist Studies* 27, 2: 361–91.

_____. 2001b. *Servants of Globalization: Women, Migration and Domestic Work*. Stanford, CA: Stanford University Press.

Patel, R. 2007. *Stuffed and Starved: Markets, Power and the Hidden Battle for the World's Food System*. London: Portobello Books.

Patwardhan, A., and J. Monro. 1982. *A Time to Rise*. National Film Board of Canada.

Philippines Women Centre of British Columbia. 2000. *Canada: The New Frontier for Filipino Mail-Order Brides*. Ottawa: Status of Women Canada.

_____. 2001. *Filipino Nurses Doing Domestic Work in Canada: A Stalled Development*. Vancouver: PWC.

Picot, G., F. Hou and S. Coulombe. 2007. *Chronic Low Income and Low-Income Dynamics Among Recent Immigrants*. Ottawa: Statistics Canada, Catalogue No. 11F0019MIE, No. 294.

Pierre, M. 2005. "Factors of Exclusion Blocking the Socioeconomic Integration of Certain Groups of Immigrant Women in Quebec. The Current State." *Nouvelles Pratiques Sociales* 17: 75–94.

Pisa, N. 2008. "Italy Declares State of Emergency over Roma Immigrants." *Daily Telegraph*. July 25. Available at <http://www.telegraph.co.uk/news/worldnews/ europe/italy/2459968/Italy-declares-state-of-emergency-over-Roma-immigrants. html> accessed September 17, 2008.

POEA (Philippine Overseas Employment Administration). 2001. POEA InfoCentre. November 5. Website. <http://www.poea.gov.ph/html/gpb.htm> accessed March 2009.

Polaski, S. 2006. "The Employment Consequences of NAFTA." Testimony submitted to the Senate Subcommittee on International Trade of the Committee on Finance. Available at <http://www.carnegieendowment.org/publications/index.cfm?fa=view&id=18703> accessed July 20, 2008.

Prashad, V. 2003. *Keeping Up With the Dow Joneses: Debt, Prison, Workfare*. Cambridge, MA: South End Press.

Pratt, G., in collaboration with Ugnayan ng Kabataang Pilipino sa Canada. 2003. "Between Homes: Displacement and Belonging for Second Generation Filipino-Canadian Youths" *B.C. Studies* 139: 41–68.

Preibisch, K.L. 2004. "Migrant Agricultural Workers and Processes of Social Inclusion in Rural Canada. *Canadian Journal of Latin American and Caribbean Studies* 29, 57/8: 203–39.

_____. 2007a. "Local Produce, Foreign Labor: Labor Mobility Programs and Global Trade Competitiveness in Canada." *Rural Sociology* 72, 3: 418–49.

_____. 2007b. "Changes in Canada's Foreign Worker Programs Serving Agriculture." Paper presented August, Montreal: Quebec Social Forum.

_____. 2007. *Patterns of Social Exclusion and Inclusion of Migrant Workers in Rural Canada*. Ottawa: The North-South Institute.

Purdy, J. 2005. "High-Tech Vegetables: Canada's Booming Greenhouse Vegetable Industry." In *VISTA on the Agri-food Industry and the Farm Community*. Catalogue no. 21- 004-XIE, March. Ottawa: Statistics Canada.

Raper, S. 2007. "Seasonal workers." Address given at Quebec Social Forum, Montreal, August.

Razack, S.H. 2004. *Dark Threats and White Knights: The Somalia Affair, Peacekeeping and the New Imperialism*. Toronto: University of Toronto Press.

_____. 2008. *Casting Out: The Eviction of Muslims from Western Law and Politics*. Toronto: University of Toronto Press.

Richmond, A.H. 1994. *Global Apartheid: Refugees, Racism and the New World Order*. Don Mills, ON: Oxford University Press.

_____. 2001. "Global Apartheid: A Postscript." *Refuge* 19, 3: 8–13.

Robington, Paul, Ann Weston and Luigi Scarpa de Masellis. 2004. "Canada's Seasonal Agricultural Workers Program as a Model of Best Practices in Migrant Worker Participation in the Benefits of Economic Globalization." Available at <http://www.nsi-ins.ca/english/research/archive/2004/05.asp> accessed January 2009.

Rodriguez, R.M. 2002. "Migrant Heroes: Nationalism, Citizenship and the Politics of Filipino Migrant Labor." *Citizenship Studies* 6, 3: 341–56.

Roque, L. 2005. "On the Losing End: The Migration of Filipino Health Professionals and the Decline of Health Care in the Philippines." Paper presented at the 10th International Metropolis Conference, Toronto, Canada, October 17–19.

Rosen, R. 2001. "Filipino Nurses in Canada." *The Canadian Women's Health Network* 4, 3.

Sassen, S. 1996. *Losing Control: Sovereignty in an Age of Globalization*. New York: Columbia University Press.

Scott, James. 1985. *Weapons of the Weak: Everyday Forms of Peasant Resistance*. New Haven, CT: Yale University Press.

Sivanandan, A. 1982. *A Different Hunger: Writings on Black Resistance*. London: Pluto Press.

Solar, Orielle, and Alec Irwin. (2007) *A Conceptual Framework for Action on the Social Determinants of Health*. Geneva: World Health Organisation (WHO) Commission on Social Determinants of Health.

Solidarity Across Borders. Website. <http://www.solidarityacrossborders.org> accessed September 17, 2008.

Spitzer, D.L., S. Bitar and M. Kalbach. 2001. "Live-In Caregivers in Alberta." Paper presented at National Metropolis Conference, Ottawa, October 17.

Spitzer, Hughes, Oxman-Martinez & Hanley. Forthcoming. *The Land of Milk & Honey?: Life after the LCP*. Funded by SSHRC.

Stasiulis, D.K., and A.B. Bakan. 2005. *Negotiating Citizenship: Migrant Women in Canada and the Global System*. Second edition. Toronto: University of Toronto Press.

_____. 1997a. "Negotiating Citizenship: The Case of Foreign Domestic Workers in Canada." *Feminist Review* 57.

_____. 1997b. *Not One of the Family: Foreign Domestic Workers in Canada*. Toronto: University of Toronto Press.

Statistics Canada. 1996. *Census: Immigration and Citizenship*.

Stephenson P.H. 1995. "Vietnamese Refugees in Victoria B.C.: An Overview of Immigrant and Refugee Health Care in a Medium-Sized Canadian Urban Centre." *Social Science and Medicine* 40

Stewart, M.J., A. Neufeld, M.J. Harrison, D. Spitzer, K. Hughes and E. Makwarimba. 2006. "Immigrant Women Family Caregivers in Canada: Implications for Policies and Programmes in Health and Social Sectors." *Health and Social Care in the Community* 14, 4: 329–40.

Sutcliffe, B. 2004. "Crossing Borders in the New Imperialism." In L. Panitch and C. Leys (eds.), *The New Imperial Challenge. Socialist Register 2004*. London: Merlin Press.

Tan, J., and P.E. Roy. 1985. "The Chinese in Canada." Booklet No. 9 of *Canada's Ethnic Groups*. Ottawa: Canadian Historical Association.

Teelucksingh, C., and G. Galabuzi. 2005. "Impact of Race and Immigrants Status on Employment Opportunities and Outcomes in the Canadian Labour Market." *Policy Matters* 22 (November). Toronto: Centre of Excellence for Research on Immigration and Settlement (CERIS).

ter Kuile, S.T., C. Rousseau, M. Munoz, L. Nadeau, M.J. Ouimet. 2007. "The Universality of the Canadian Health Care System in Question: Barriers to Services for Immigrants and Refugees." *International Journal of Migration, Health and Social Care* 3, 1: 15–26.

Thobani, S. 2000. "Nationalizing Canadians: Bordering Immigrant Women in the Late Twentieth Century." *Canadian Journal of Women and the Law* 12, 2: 279–312.

_____. 2007. *Exalted Subjects: Studies in the Making of Race and Nation in Canada*. Toronto: University of Toronto Press.

Tran, K., and T. Chui. 2005. *Longitudinal Survey of Immigrants to Canada: Progress and Challenges of New Immigrants in the Workforce 2003*. Statistics Canada.

_____. 2006. *Longitudinal Survey of Immigrants to Canada: A Regional Perspective of the Labour Market Experiences 2003*. Statistics Canada.

United Nations, Department of Economic and Social Affairs, Population Division. 2007. "World Population Prospects: The 2006 Revision, Highlights." Working paper No. ESA/P/WP.202. Available at <http://www.un.org/esa/population/

publications/wpp2006/WPP2006_Highlights_rev.pdf> accessed January 2009.

Velasco, P. 2002. "Filipino Migrant Workers Amidst Globalization." *Canadian Woman Studies* 22, 1: 131–35.

Weston, A. 2007. *The Changing Economic Context for Canada's Seasonal Agricultural Workers Program*. Research Report. Ottawa: The North-South Institute.

Weston, A., and L. Scarpa de Masellis. 2003. *Hemispheric Integration and Trade Relations — Implications for Canada's Seasonal Agricultural Workers Program. Research Report.* Ottawa: The North-South Institute.

Wise, T. 2007. "Policy Space for Mexican Maize: Protecting Agro-Diodiversity by Promoting Rural Livelihoods." February. Global Development and Environment Institute at Tufts University. Available at <http://www.ase.tufts.edu/gdae/policy_research/MexicanMaize.html> accessed May 13, 2008.

Zaman, H. 2004. "Transnational Migration and Commodification of Im/Migrant Female Laborers in Canada." *International Journal of Canadian Studies* 28: 41–62.

Zanchetta, M.S.,and I.M. Poureslami. 2006. "Health Literacy Within the Reality of Immigrants' Culture and Language." *Canadian Journal of Public Health* 97: S26–S30.

Legislation and Conventions

Act Respecting Labour Standards. 1980. Commission du norms de travail, Gouvernement de Quebec.

Canada Health Act. R.S.C. 1985: c. C-6.

Canada-U.S. Safe Third Country Agreement. 2004. Available at Citizenship and Immigration Canada website <http://www.cic.gc.ca/ENGLISH/department/laws-policy/menu-safethird.asp> accessed January 2009.

Canadian Charter of Rights and Freedoms. 1982. Department of Justice, Government of Canada.

Chinese Immigration Act. 1885. C. 71: An Act to Restrict and Regulate Chinese Immigration into Canada. [Assented to July 20, 1855.]

Immigration and Refugee Protection Act. 2002. C. 27. Current to January 23, 2009. Minister of Justice Canada.

Security and Prosperity Partnership of North America. Available at <http://www.spp.gov> accessed January 2009.

United Nations High Commission for Human Rights (UNHCHR). 1966. International Covenant on Economic, Social and Cultural Rights (CESCR). Adopted and opened for signature, ratification and accession by General Assemply resolution 2200A (XXI) of December 16, 1966; entry into force January 3, 1976, in accordance with article 27.

_____. 1990. International Convention on the Protection of the Rights of all Migrant Workers and Members of Their Families (CPRMWMF). Adopted by General Assembly resolution 45/158 of December 18, 1990.

Jurisprudence

Dunmore v. Ontario (Attorney-General), [2001] 3 S.C.R 1016.